# PARADOX AND PLATITUDE IN
# WITTGENSTEIN'S PHILOSOPHY

# Paradox and Platitude in Wittgenstein's Philosophy

DAVID PEARS

CLARENDON PRESS · OXFORD

# OXFORD
UNIVERSITY PRESS

Great Clarendon Street, Oxford OX2 6DP

Oxford University Press is a department of the University of Oxford.
It furthers the University's objective of excellence in research, scholarship,
and education by publishing worldwide in

Oxford New York

Auckland Cape Town Dar es Salaam Hong Kong Karachi
Kuala Lumpur Madrid Melbourne Mexico City Nairobi
New Delhi Shanghai Taipei Toronto

With offices in

Argentina Austria Brazil Chile Czech Republic France Greece
Guatemala Hungary Italy Japan Poland Portugal Singapore
South Korea Switzerland Thailand Turkey Ukraine Vietnam

Oxford is a registered trade mark of Oxford University Press
in the UK and in certain other countries

Published in the United States
by Oxford University Press Inc., New York

British Library Cataloguing in Publication Data

Data available

Library of Congress Cataloging in Publication Data

Data available

Typeset by Laserwords Private Limited, Chennai, India
Printed in Great Britain
on acid-free paper by
Biddles Ltd, King's Lynn, Norfolk

ISBN 0-19-924770-6  978-0-19-924770-7

1 3 5 7 9 10 8 6 4 2

To Isaiah Berlin

# Preface

If an anthropologist from outer space visited our planet in order to write an account of our lives, the activity that would probably give him most trouble would be philosophy. Does it explore the world like a science, but in a deeper and more general way? Or does it only examine our own thinking about the world? And why is the object onto which it is most sharply focused so often only itself? These questions are difficult enough to answer, but what the visitor would find even harder to understand is that they never get final answers. The history of philosophy reveals a pattern, but it is a pattern of oscillation between two very different endeavours: expansive exploration and anxious self-criticism. Philosophy, we could tell our visitor, is like a pulsar. Wittgenstein's work belongs to a critical phase in the history of the subject, Kant inaugurated another, earlier critical phase, and Socrates' shrewd dismantling of the received ideas of his contemporaries is our earliest example of this kind of philosophy.

Naturally, these two phases often overlap one another and there is nothing to stop them coexisting within a single school of philosophers, or even within the mind of a single philosopher. We might try to explain this by saying that critical philosophy is needed to sharpen the tools that are used by constructive philosophy. But this reconciliation leaves out something very important. It fails to mention that constructive philosophy has often claimed to explore a field of its own, like the world explored by the natural sciences but somehow beyond it, and that is a claim that critical philosophy since the time of Kant has strenuously rejected.

This produces a tension within contemporary philosophy, a tension which is its dominant feature. We feel that the only way to explain and justify our own modes of thought is to move beyond them to find the support that they seem to need. But where is there for us to go? So we return empty-handed, or, perhaps, with only too many empty words, and we try instead to justify our thinking on its own ground and in its own terms. But would that really be justification? Would it not merely be a description of autonomous patterns of thought? And why should we allow philosophy to act as judge in its own case?

This tension is the dominant topic of the five chapters that follow. They trace its impact on Wittgenstein's philosophy in three areas: meaning, logic, and persons. They deal not only with what he wrote but also with the philosophical context of his writings. They also include the effect that he intended his writings to have on us and their actual effect. We have to remember that, like Socrates, he treated philosophy as a very personal discipline. You ought to give your immediate reaction to questions like 'What preserves the meanings of words?' or 'What makes logical inferences compelling?' Then you should submit your answer to a dialectical critique which will test it by applying it to other similar cases and hammer it into a more convincing shape, or, perhaps, demonstrate that it is not worth preserving even in a modified form. You should never ride rough-shod over exceptions or show contempt for the particular case (see Wittgenstein: *The Blue Book*, pp. 17–20).

So far, this might be a description of Socrates' procedure in Plato's early dialogues. But at this point a big difference emerges. Socrates was looking for convincing definitions of the virtues, but Wittgenstein believed that definitions always miss their target, whatever it might be. The explanation of their failure is that words are like living organisms and they develop new meanings and lose their old meanings or have them modified.[1] If a philosopher like Socrates or Plato tries to freeze them onto the universals that he takes them to signify, the explanation of their meaning will be too rigid and incompatible with further developments. What is more, it will be a circular explanation, because the universals will be identifiable only through their links with the words.

This last objection—that the Realist's explanation of the meanings of words is circular—is the key to understanding Wittgenstein's critical philosophy. It is used quite generally in *Philosophical Investigations* (*PI*) against any theory that tries to base constancy of meaning on a feature of the world that turns out not to be independent of our techniques of applying words to things. If it is valid, it will destroy both Realism and

---

[1] Wittgenstein emphasizes not only the multifariousness of the things to which a single word is applied (often they are related by something more like family resemblances than a common property (*PI* I, S 67)) but also the importance of innovations (*PI* I, S 18) So if we seek unity in the technique of applying the word, we shall often find that the technique itself is changeable (see Ch. 2). The plasticity of linguistic techniques plays an important role in Wittgenstein's account of logical necessity (see Ch. 4). Linguistic techniques are essentially plastic or volatile.

Gilbert Ryle, whose philosophy owes much to discussions with Wittgenstein, makes a related but more limited use of the concept of a linguistic technique (see *The Concept of Mind*, Ch. II, 'Knowing How and Knowing That').

Nominalism, not because they are mistaken theories but simply because they are theories. So it will eliminate the pictorial theory of sentences, which had been the central pillar of the *Tractatus*, and in the end we shall be left without any theories. What we shall have instead is only the point of view that Hao Wang called 'anthropologism'.

The point is made very forcefully in *Philosophical Investigations*:

> And we may not advance any kind of theory. There must not be anything hypothetical in our considerations. We must do away with all *explanation*, and description alone must take its place. And this description gets its light, that is to say its purpose, from the philosophical problems. These are, of course, not empirical problems; they are solved, rather, by looking into the workings of our language, and that in such a way as to make us recognize those workings: *in despite of* an urge to misunderstand them. The problems are solved not by giving new information, but by arranging what we have always known. Philosophy is a battle against the bewitchment of our intelligence by means of language.   (*PI* I, S 109)

Many people find this unsatisfying. It is natural to assume that, if something that we do conforms to a standard, that standard must be independent of our performance. Wittgenstein's rejection of this plausible assumption is highly paradoxical. How can what we do show us what we ought to do? Surely whatever we do must have a goal and we shall have to discover the means of achieving it and there ought to be a theory telling us what the right means would be. How can there be any exceptions to this general pattern? How can our thought and language possibly have *internal* standards of correctness? The very idea seems to be incoherent, because it looks as if an activity that created its own standards of correctness as it went along would not really have any standards but would just be capricious. We should all be like Humpty-Dumpty, who said 'It's my word and I can do what I like with it.'

This is the central paradox of Wittgenstein's later philosophy. But he does not meet it head-on by providing an alternative theory about the correct use of words or about the compulsiveness of logical inference. He only gives us an oblique response to it by reminding us of familiar examples of correctness or validity. What he tells us is flat and platitudinous—it has no theoretical depth and it is what we already knew. So, of course, it is not controversial. The controversial point is the claim that he makes for this kind of reminder: it is enough in itself without the reinforcement of any philosophical theory.

This deeply anti-theoretical philosophy was anathema to Bertrand Russell, who had admired, even if he had not been convinced by, Wittgenstein's early work.[2] But this is not a matter of taste or upbringing. If Wittgenstein's critical philosophy is misguided, that can only be because his ideas about meaning are too restrictive and because the point at which he saw his opponent's theories vanish in the void of meaninglessness was too near home.

This book is based on the conviction that the tension between critical and constructive philosophy cannot be resolved by general arguments. If neither of the two adversaries can be disqualified in advance, we can only observe them in action and see how they fare. So in Chapters 2–5 Wittgenstein's contributions to four controversial topics are examined in detail, while in Chapter 1 his own early theory of meaning, soon to be abandoned, is introduced as an object of comparison.

The number of books and articles on Wittgenstein's philosophy is vast, and in this book no attempt has been made to record all debts and disagreements. Even the connections with my own past work, positive and negative, are not given in detail. However, there is one connection which can be recorded briefly. In 1971 I published a short monograph on Wittgenstein in which I characterized him as the great critical philosopher of the twentieth century[3] and I was surprised and pleased when Stravinsky wrote to tell me that the book had given him pleasure.

This book, begun at the Rockafeller Centre, Bellagio in 2001, covers much the same ground in greater depth and detail, and it is written with the same conviction that the structure of Wittgenstein's ideas and the connections between them owe much to an imagination that is essential to philosophy but can so very easily lead us nowhere.

---

[2] See B. Russell, *My Philosophical Development* (Allen & Unwin, 1959, 216–17): 'The earlier Wittgenstein, whom I knew intimately, was a man addicted to passionately intense thinking, profoundly aware of difficult problems of which I, like him, felt the importance, and possessed (or at least so I thought) of true philosophical genius. The later Wittgenstein, on the contrary, seems to have grown tired of serious thinking and to have invented a doctrine which would make such an activity unnecessary. I do not for one moment believe that the doctrine which has these lazy consequences is true. I realize, however, that I have an overpoweringly strong bias against it, for, if it is true, philosophy is, at best, a slight help to lexicographers, and at worst, an idle tea-table amusement.'

[3] See my *Wittgenstein* Fontana, Modern Masters, ed. Frank Kermode, (Fontana–Collins, 1971).

Texts cited from Wittgenstein's writings are quoted in their published English translations except in cases where I have found it necessary to alter them, and then the alteration is recorded in a footnote.

Finally, I would like to express my gratitude to Elsie Hinkes, who has deciphered the handwritten text of this book so perceptively, and to Professor Naomi Eilan who gave invaluable help with the later stages of the production of this book.

New York,
December 2004

# Contents

# 1

# The Pictorial Character of Language

If a traveller in a foreign country could neither speak nor understand its language, he could at least make himself understood by sketching pictures of what he needed, or of his destination, or of the place from which he came. That is a fact and it suggests a theory: perhaps a sentence really is a kind of picture. That was the theory that Wittgenstein developed in his first book, *Tractatus Logico-Philosophicus*, but abandoned in his later writings.

The theory gave a Realist answer to the question 'How does a sentence achieve a sense that can be communicated from speaker to hearer?' The answer was that the words stand for things and the temporal or spatial arrangement of the words in a sentence represents the actual arrangement of the things in the world. If the things really are arranged as the pattern of the words says that they are,—if, for example, that house really does have a fanlight over the front door—then the sentence is true, but, if not, it is false. This simple answer offers a Realist explanation of sense: the world is the dominant partner in its relations with language and sentences achieve senses because their words represent possible arrangements of things in the world.

Someone who was not too fussy about details might find the general idea of this explanation vaguely convincing. But Wittgenstein did care about details and he tried to work them out in the *Tractatus*. This chapter will describe the emergence of the Picture Theory in the early phase of his philosophy. The general idea developed in the theory is that a verbal description of a scene is like the surface of a pointillist painting: each dot stands for a particular point in space and the colour of the dot conveys a message about that point, and thus the whole painting is a complicated report of the actual scene. So Seurat's work 'La Grande Jatte' is like a complex verbal description of what he saw on that summer's day, and, if we take the next step, a verbal description is itself another kind of picture.

When Wittgenstein was working out the details of this theory in the *Tractatus*, and more perspicuously in *Notebooks 1914–1916*, (the journal in which the ideas of the *Tractatus* were first developed) there was one question that he did not press: what *sort* of explanation of meaning did the theory provide? Now a typical scientific explanation of a phenomenon would indicate its cause and the cause would have to be something that could be identified independently of the effect. For example, thunder is caused by a discharge of electricity from sky to earth and that is a cause that can be identified independently of the thunder that is the effect. So Molière mocks the doctor who says that his medicine induces sleep because it has a soporific power. That is like saying that someone is popular because people like him. Of course, these remarks are true, but they do not offer scientific explanations and that raises the question, whether they have any explanatory power of any kind or merely paraphrase the original statements by spelling out the meanings of the words 'soporific' or 'popular'.

This question is evaded by Realists. In Plato's *Republic* Socrates says that, when things have the same name, they share the same Form (*Rep.* 596A). However, he does not offer any way of identifying the Form independently of its effect on the way people describe the things that share it. He seems to assume that the problem is epistemological and that the right training would sharpen our intellects and give them the acuity required to perceive Forms directly. But really it is a logical problem, which surfaces at many points in the history of philosophy, and nowhere more conspicuously than in the development of Wittgenstein's philosophy.

In the *Tractatus* Wittgenstein simply assumes that the world is the dominant partner in its relations with language. I call this flower blue because I recognize that that is its colour. True enough, but my statement owed its sense to the previous correlation of the word with the colour, and it is not so easy to see how that correlation should be characterized. The difficulty is that, if the specification of the colour is going to reflect the way in which we actually apply the colour-word, it will have to use the colour-word and say that the word 'blue' is correlated with the colour blue. But that is too like the doctor's specification of the medicine that helps his patients to sleep because it has a soporific power.

It might be thought that this objection to the Picture Theory and to other Realist theories of meaning is captious. For, in many cases, we can do what compilers of dictionaries do: we can define the word in question. True, it may not be possible to define the word 'blue'—at least, not in a way that will reflect how people recognize when to apply it—but in many other cases it will be possible. However, that would only be a temporary evasion of the difficulty, because the words used in the definitions would themselves have to be applied to things. Sooner or later we must reach the interface between language and the world and at that point it will not be possible to characterize the correlations of words with things in an informative way (*PI* I, S 201). Wittgenstein has a vivid way of describing what happens then—we begin to stammer [*PI* I, S 433]—and, as Molière saw, we stammer because we no longer have an explanatory theory. We can, of course, demonstrate the application of words to things, but that will not explain it: explanations must use more words.

Once this point has been made, it is so obvious that it may seem surprising that empty Realism has been so persistent in the history of ideas. The reason must be that a flat rejection of Realism will always have an air of paradox. If the world is not the dominant partner in its relationship with language, what else will provide our sentences with their senses? The answer that Wittgenstein gave to that question in his later writings was 'What we do with them'. But that has an air of platitude. Of course it is what we do with them. But what is that if it is not that we attach the words to definite, identifiable sets of things in the world? But are they *independently* identifiable? That is the question that has to be asked by anyone who wants to understand the development of Wittgenstein's philosophy. It was always obvious to him that Realism did not offer a scientific explanation of the phenomenon of meaning, but he did not immediately see that it did not offer a genuine explanation of any kind.

This problem will be discussed in more detail in the next chapter. Wittgenstein's reaction to it was to abandon his Realist theory of meaning and to develop in its place a very different account of the correlation of words with things, or, to put it in his way, of linguistic regularity (usually called 'following a rule'). The new account is anthropocentric without being subjective, and its cardinal concept is the concept of an incompletely formulatable linguistic technique. Solon once said that no man should be called happy until he was dead, and Wittgenstein applied his idea to the careers of words. While a word remains in use, its application may develop in ways that cannot be anticipated, and so no account of its use can have the finality of an obituary. But that can wait: the topic of this chapter is the theory that a sentence is a kind of picture.

There are three preliminary points that need to be made about this theory before it is examined in detail. First, the objection that it is a theory without any explanatory power was not Wittgenstein's only reason for abandoning it, but it was his deepest reason. Second, that it is an objection not only to Realism but also to its traditional rival, Nominalism. For when the Nominalist relies on the similarity between the particular things to which a general word is applicable, he is obliged to specify the similarity that he means, just as the Realist was obliged to specify the Form or universal that he meant. The third preliminary point can be made by asking a question: if the need for an independent specification of the extension of a general word is so obvious, how can Wittgenstein have overlooked it?

But he did not overlook it. He relied on his enigmatic doctrine of showing to deal with it:

A proposition *shows* its sense.
A proposition *shows* how things stand *if* it is true.
And it *says that* they do so stand.   (*TLP*, 4.022)

The distinction between saying and showing maps onto the difference between contingent and necessary propositions. It is, of course, a contingent proposition that in a given language a particular sound or shape is correlated with a particular object, but the proposition that a particular *name* is correlated with a particular object is not contingent. For the word ranks as a name only because of that correlation.

A name means an object. The object is its meaning.   (*TLP*, 3.203)

If we cannot *say* that a particular name means a particular object but only *show* that it does by actually applying it to that object, the same restriction will apply to a group of names in a sentence, and that is why a sentence can only show its sense. This is connected with the point just made about explanations of meaning: I cannot explain the meaning of the word 'mauve' by saying that it means the colour '*mauve*' because that would be using the correlation that it was supposed to explain instead of giving an independent identification of the colour.

Some commentators argue that in the *Tractatus*, when Wittgenstein says that something can only be shown and not said, what is shown is intended to be unintelligible rather than merely lacking in factual sense—a ladder to be thrown away after we have climbed it and attained sophistication[1] (or, as Sextus said when he had used that image, an emetic which voids itself with the problematic food. (Sextus Empiricus, *Adversus Mathematicos*, II, 480–1)). It is unlikely that Wittgenstein had reached that point when he compiled the *Tractatus*. But even if he had reached it, he certainly had not applied it destructively to the Picture Theory of sentences. For he never admits that there is a flaw that vitiates the whole theory: neither the objects designated by names nor their possibilities of combination are independently identifiable, and so the theory does not yield a genuine explanation of meaning. On the contrary, the theory serves as the foundation of the whole system of the *Tractatus*.[2]

It is a beautiful theory and it can be appreciated by anyone who is willing to postpone consideration of its ultimate fate. What it has

---

[1] Cora Diamond interprets Wittgenstein's use of the concept of showing in the *Tractatus* in this way (see her article, 'Throwing away the Ladder', *Philosophy*, 1988, repr. in Cora Diamond, *The Realistic Spirit* (MIT Press, 1995)). Cf. James Conant, The Method of the *Tractatus*, in Erich Reck (ed.), *From Frege to Wittgenstein: Perspectives on Early Analytic Philosophy* (Oxford, 2000) and reprinted with other articles taking much the same line in Alice Crary and Rupert Read (eds.), *The New Wittgenstein* (Routledge, 2000).

[2] On 19 Aug. 1919 Wittgenstein wrote to Russell from Cassino answering questions that he had asked about the *Tractatus* after reading it for the first time. Russell must have asked why the number of objects can only be shown by the number of names. Wittgenstein replies: 'This touches the cardinal question of what can be expressed by a prop [*sic*] and what cannot be expressed but only shown. I can't explain at length here. Just think that what you want to *say* by the apparent proposition "There are 2 things" is shown by there being two names which have different meanings (or by there being one name which may have two meanings).' It is impossible to believe that, when he wrote this, what he meant was that the sentence 'There are two things' not only lacks factual sense but also fails in a more radical way—there is nothing that it is even trying to say. His point is only that the information is being conveyed in the wrong way. For 'There are two things' is only an apparent proposition and 'thing' is only a pseudo-concept (cf. *TLP*, 4. 1272). The right way to express it is simply to use the two names and so to show what cannot be said.

Similarly, it is impossible to believe that in the opening sections of *Notes Dictated to G. E. Moore in Norway* (now reprinted in *Notebooks 1914–1916*), his extensive use of the concept of *showing* was made 'with his tongue in his cheek' and nothing in his mind—i.e., with nothing that is apprehended by the naïve ladder-climber.

It is far more plausible to suppose that there was a radical change in his account of meaning and that the tension that led to the change can already be felt in the final propositions of the *Tractatus*. Unfortunately, the *Notebooks* version of them, if there was one, has not survived. It might have been revealing.

We have a natural tendency to suppose that future events cast their shadows on the present. The infant Jesus is sometimes represented with a crucifix hanging from his neck and when we analyse the development of complex ideas in a philosopher's mind, it is especially easy to allow later features to be given an earlier date. See Ch. 2 pp. 30–36 for a general discussion of this tendency.

to explain is the miracle of sense. The individual words in a sentence correspond to things that actually exist—they are like stakes driven into the ground—but the whole sentence only corresponds to a possibility which may not be realized. Indeed, the point of a sentence is to take a flight from reality, not by saying something false but by saying something that, even if it is true, might have been false. But how does this heavier-than-air machine stay up?[3] It is not enough that the individual words should correspond to real things, and it would be too much to require that the whole sentence should correspond to a realized possibility, because that would give it a sense only if it was true. The very most that we can require is that it should correspond to a real possibility. But what is that?

In *Notebooks 1914–1916*, there is a series of entries in which Wittgenstein is struggling with the problem of sense, and eventually comes out with the Picture Theory as we have it in the *Tractatus* (*Notebooks*, October–November 1914). It would not be a great exaggeration to say that, if we did not have this record of work in progress, but only the announcement of the result in the *Tractatus*, we would not be able to understand the theory. In the entries in the *Notebooks* he formulates the condition that must be satisfied by any successful solution to the problem of sense.

The knowledge of the representing relation *must* be founded on the knowledge of the component parts of the situation   (*NB*, 3-xi-14)

This is repeated a few weeks later:

The reality that corresponds to the sense of the proposition can surely be nothing but its component parts, since we are surely *ignorant* of *everything* else   (*NB*, 20-xi-14)

If we have any knowledge of a possibility, it must be based on our knowledge of the things that have the possibility—i.e., the things for which the individual words in a sentence stand. But what kind of knowledge is that supposed to be?

The way to get an answer to that question is to look at the stage that had been reached in this part of the philosophy of language in 1912, when Wittgenstein first entered the field. His greatest debts, as he says in the Preface to the *Tractatus*, were to Frege and Russell, and

---

[3] This was Isaiah Berlin's characterization of the question that Wittgenstein's Picture Theory was designed to answer.

the Picture Theory is a critical response to some of Russell's ideas. Now Russell's account of understanding a sentence underwent many changes in the first two decades of the twentieth century, but throughout them all it remained based on his concept of knowledge by acquaintance. He maintained that acquaintance with a thing is prior to, and independent of, any knowledge of its nature, and so prior to, and independent of, any knowledge of its possible properties or its possible relations with other things. Wittgenstein flatly disagreed with this:

'If I know' (German: kennen) 'an object, I also know all its possible occurrences in states of affairs.'
   (Every one of these possibilities must be part of the nature of the object.)
   A new possibility cannot be discovered later.   (*TLP*, 2.0123)

This expansion of the scope of acquaintance is the key to understanding the Picture Theory. For it naturally led to a corresponding expansion of the concept of *standing for*. When a word is correlated with an object, that will no longer be enough to ensure that it stands for it. It will also be necessary that the word be combined with other words only in ways that reflect the possibilities of combination of its object with their objects. Things have elective affinities which must be matched by the words that stand for them. A colour cannot be pungent and a smell cannot be yellow.

These two modifications of Russell's doctrines, one epistemic and the other semantic, swiftly produced the solution to the problem of sense. It is set out in two days' entries in November 1914 in the *Notebooks*:

One name is representative of one thing, another of another thing, and they themselves are connected; in this way the whole images the situation—like a *tableau vivant*.
   The logical connection must, of course, be one that is possible as between the things that the names are representatives of, and this will always be the case if the names really are representatives of the things. N.B. that connection is not a relation but only the *holding* of a relation.
   In this way the proposition represents the situation—as it were off its own bat.
   But when I say: the connection of the propositional components must be possible for the represented things—does this not contain the whole problem? How can a non-existent connection between objects be possible?
   'The connection must be possible' means:
   The proposition and the components of the situation must stand in a particular relation.

Then in order for a proposition to present a situation, it is only necessary for its component parts to represent those of the situation and for the former to stand in a relation which is possible for the latter.   (*NB*, 4 and 5-xi-14)

These entries bring out the true force of the Picture Theory far more clearly than the oracular version that Wittgenstein published in the *Tractatus*. It is a Realist theory because it treats objects as the dominant partners in their relationship with words and it does so in two distinct ways. First, a word acquired its meaning when it was correlated with an object, because the object then *became* its meaning (see *TLP*, 3.203, quoted above, p. 4). Second, less obviously, a word keeps its meaning only so long as its occurrences in sentences track the object's possibilities of combination with other objects:

If all objects are given, then at the same time all *possible* states of affairs are given.

Each thing is, as it were, in a space of possible states of affairs. This space I can imagine empty, but I cannot imagine the thing without the space.   (*TLP*, 2.0124–2.013)

That specifies the essential connection between objects and their possibilities of combination with other objects.

It is only in the nexus of an elementary proposition that a name occurs in a proposition.   (*TLP*, 4.23)

This adaptation of Frege's Context Principle requires that names be introduced only in connection with other names in elementary propositions.

The message of the Picture Theory, as it is spelled out in the *Notebooks*, is uncompromisingly Realist. Words stand for the objects that are their meanings, but they stand for them only so long as their combinations represent combinations that are possible for those objects. That is the deeper level at which sentences have to fit possibilities in order to acquire and preserve their senses. After that they can acquire truth at the more obvious level when the possibilities are realized as facts.

It must be admitted that this message does not come across so clearly in the long passage in the *Tractatus* in which Wittgenstein introduces the Picture Theory (*TLP*, 2.1–2.19). This might be because there had been a change of doctrine between the time when he made the entries in the *Notebooks* and the time when he compiled the *Tractatus*. Alternatively, the difference might only be a difference in perspicuity produced by a difference in terminology.

In fact, the terminology used by Wittgenstein in the *Tractatus* does have a feature that helps to explain the greater obscurity of the definitive version of the Picture Theory. In the *Notebooks* the theory is based on the concept of isomorphic possibility: the combinability of names in a sentence must reflect the combinability in reality of the objects designated by the names. In the *Tractatus* the concept of *Form* is used to express the same requirement, which is now formulated like this: sentence and state of affairs must have the same form. Since form is defined in the *Tractatus* as 'the possibility of structure' (*TLP*, 2.033), this formulation is only another version of the requirement imposed in the *Notebooks*, but it does make the exposition of the Picture Theory harder to follow. We can immediately grasp the basic idea that the words in a sentence must be combined in ways that map onto the possibilities available to the objects for which they stand, but the requirement loses its immediate clarity when the word 'form' is used to express it.

What any picture, of whatever form must have in common with reality in order to be able to depict it—correctly or incorrectly—in any way at all, is logical form, i.e. the form of reality. (*TLP*, 2.18)

If we are going to understand this version of the requirement, we have to remember that form is the possibility of structure, and so a picture and the reality that it depicts will share the same form when the arrangement of the elements in the picture presents a possible arrangement of the correlated elements in reality. That is the central point of the Picture Theory.

There is also another peculiarity of the exposition of the theory in the *Tractatus* which makes it more difficult to understand than the earlier exposition in the *Notebooks*. When Wittgenstein introduces form in the *Tractatus* as 'the possibility of structure', it is immediately obvious that there are different kinds of possibility and so that there are different kinds of form. The two most important kinds in the exposition of the Picture Theory are spatial possibility and logical possibility. A map exploits spatial possibility and a sentence exploits logical possibility. So the Picture Theory can be seen as a generalization of the requirement of shared form from the homogeneous case in which the possibility is spatial (the map) to the heterogeneous case in which the possibility is only logical (the sentence).

This may not be immediately intelligible and there are two things that make it hard to grasp. One is the fact that spatial possibility is a species of logical possibility and so, though a map is specifically a spatial picture, it is also generically a logical picture.

Every picture is *at the same time* a logical one. (On the other hand not every picture is, for example, a spatial one.) (*TLP*, 2.182)

However, though a map is generically a logical picture, we do not call it a logical picture but reserve that description for sentences, because the possibilities exploited by sentences cannot be described in any more specific way.

A picture whose pictorial form is logical form is called a logical picture. (*TLP*, 2.181)

The second thing that makes this theory hard to grasp is not the complexity of the classification of shared forms but something much more central. We do not immediately see how Wittgenstein manages to generalize his concept of shared form from the homogeneous case (the map), where it is obvious, to the heterogeneous case (the sentence), where it is less obvious.

Maps are paradigms of picturing. But if someone whistled the song of a bird, that would be an auditory homogeneous picture, and if he recorded it on a tape, the pattern of magnetization would be a visual heterogeneous picture. So Wittgenstein says later:

A gramophone record, the musical idea, the written notes and the sound-waves, all stand to one another in the same internal relation of depicting that holds between language and the world. (*TLP*, 4.014)

The relation of depicting surfaces in unexpected examples of isomorphism, but it is best to start with the investigation of paradigmatic cases.

So what do we learn from paradigmatic cases? First, we find that a picture must have as many distinguishable parts as there are in the situation that it represents (*TLP*, 404). But though this equal multiplicity is a necessary condition of successful picturing, it is not a sufficient condition. For, as Wittgenstein insists in his exposition in the *Notebooks*, it is also necessary that the elements of the picture should be combined in ways that represent possible configurations of the things for which they stand. Now it is only marginally possible for a spatial picture to violate this condition (for example, it is violated by some of Escher's work), but it is easy for a string of words to violate it. This is because there is a difference between the way in which a homogeneous picture, like a map, gets its sense and the way in which a heterogeneous picture, like a sentence, gets its sense. A map is set up by a method of projection that settles the correlation of points in the picture with points on the ground in a single package deal, but the sense of a sentence depends on the individual correlations of its words with the things for which they stand. So a map's preservation of its sense is a general and largely automatic achievement, while the preservation of the sense of a sentence owes more to our vigilance and attention to the meanings of the individual words.

The exposition of the Picture Theory in *Tractatus*, 2.18–2.182 is intended to show that, from a logical point of view, this difference is superficial. The important thing is that both maps and verbal messages have to present real possibilities and the differences between the ways in which they satisfy this requirement—the map by its scale, orientation, and point of origin, and the verbal message by a long list of independent linguistic conventions—are merely distractions which make it hard for us to see that they share the same pictorial character.

So, of course, his exposition ought to start from a homogeneous case where the medium is spatial. But he does not mention this kind of case until his exposition is well advanced.

A picture can depict any reality whose form it has.

A spatial picture can depict anything spatial, a coloured one, anything coloured, etc.   (*TLP*, 2.171)

This ought to have been the starting-point of his exposition, because the idea was to generalize the concept of shared form (i.e., shared possibility of structure) from homogeneous cases, where it is obvious, to heterogeneous cases, where it is not obvious.

Incidentally, the text just quoted does not imply that spatial information can only be conveyed by a spatial picture or that a spatial picture can only convey spatial information. The point is only that in homogeneous cases the sharing of form is more easily understood and so its intuitive appeal is maximized when both medium and object are spatial.

All this would have been easier to understand if it had been preceded by the explicit requirement that, if words are going to stand for objects, they must be combined only in ways that present combinations that are possible for those objects. But this requirement does not get a separate formulation in the *Tractatus*. Instead, it is left implicit in the requirement that a picture must share the form of the reality that it represents.

What any picture, of whatever form, must have in common with reality, in order to be able to depict it—correctly or incorrectly—in any way at all, is logical form, i.e. the form of reality.   (*TLP*, 2.18)

Here we have to remember his definition of form: Form is 'the possibility of structure' (*TLP*, 2.033).

We now have a detailed account of the Picture Theory, but what was the point of it? Evidently, there are similarities between sentences and spatial pictures used to convey information, but why was that so important? In order to answer that question, we need to know the circumstances of its origin and the nature of the problem that it was designed to solve. Fortunately, this information is available.

Wittgenstein's Picture Theory was developed as an alternative to Russell's two main theories of judgement, the first of which was published in 1910,[4] while the second was formulated in 1913 but not published until 1984.[5]

Both theories were criticized by Wittgenstein, and the second one was Russell's response to his criticisms of the first one. Wittgenstein did not find the response convincing. There is a letter from Russell to Lady Ottoline Morrell dated 28 May 1913 in which he reports the fact that Wittgenstein had criticized the book that he was writing (*Theory of Knowledge, 1913*), but does not give the details of the criticism.

We were both cross from the heat. I showed him a crucial part of what I have been writing. He said it was all wrong, not realizing the difficulties—that he had tried my view and knew it wouldn't work. I couldn't understand his objection—in fact he was very inarticulate—but I feel in my bones that he must be right, and that he had seen something that I have missed. If I could see it too, I shouldn't mind, but as it is, it is worrying, and has rather destroyed the pleasure in my writing—I can only go on with what I see, and yet I feel it is probably all wrong, and that Wittgenstein will probably think me a dishonest scoundrel for going on with it. Well, well,—it is the younger generation knocking at the door—I must make room for him when I can, or I shall become an incubus. But at the moment I was rather cross.    (Quoted by R. W. Clark, *The Life of Bertrand Russell*, Jonathan Caps and Weidenfeld & Nicolson, London, 1975 pp. 204–5)

What Wittgenstein found unsatisfactory in *Theory of Knowledge 1913* must have been Russell's new theory of judgement. In June 1913 in a letter to Russell he writes:

I can now express my objection to your theory of judgement exactly: I believe it is obvious that from the proposition 'A judges that (say) a is in a relation R

---

[4] 'On the Nature of Truth and Falsehood', in B. Russell, *Mysticism and Logic and Other Essays*. (London: Longmans Green & Co., 1921).

[5] B. Russell, *Theory of Knowledge 1913*, ed. E. Eames and K. Blackwell in *The Collected Papers of Bertrand Russell*, Vol. 7 (London: Allen & Unwin, 1984).

to b', if correctly analysed, the proposition 'aRb ∨∼ aRb' must follow directly *without the use of any other premiss*. This condition is not fulfilled by your theory.    (*Notebooks 1914–1916*, Appendix III, p. 121.)

In July he writes:

I am very sorry to hear that my objection to your theory of judgement paralyses you. I think it can only be removed by a correct theory of propositions.    (Ibid.)

These are criticisms of Russell's second theory of judgement developed in *Theory of Knowledge 1913*, which Wittgenstein first saw in May 1913. But in Wittgenstein's *Notes on Logic*, which was probably completed before that date, there is a similar criticism of Russell's first theory of judgement.

Every right theory of judgement must make it impossible to judge that 'This table penholders the book'. (Russell's theory does not satisfy this requirement.) (*Notebooks 1914–1916*, Appendix I; *Notes on Logic* 96)

These criticisms are episodes in a running battle between the two philosophers. Wittgenstein's complaint, expressed briefly in the last one, is that Russell's first theory allowed a person to judge something nonsensical, but that would not be judgement. This is a fair criticism of Russell's first theory, which was an attempt to base sense on acquaintance with objects, interpreted extensionally, and so without any knowledge of their possibilities of combination with one another. As Wittgenstein observes in the letter that he wrote to Russell in July 1914, this fault 'can only be removed by a correct theory of propositions', and he did not agree that the theory that Russell used to remove it in *Theory of Knowledge 1913* was correct.

We know that Wittgenstein tried to solve this problem by making acquaintance intensional, and maintaining that a word stands for an object only so long as it respects its possibilities of combination with other objects. (See above, p. 8). Russell's remedy, developed in *Theory of Knowledge 1913*, was much more elaborate. He continued to treat acquaintance as an extensional relation, and he suggested that, in order to understand the proposition, '$\phi a$' I must be acquainted not only with the property, $\phi$, and the particular, $a$, but also with a logical object,[6] the general form of monadic propositions, $\xi$ x. My acquaintance with

---

[6] According to Russell, the logical constants also denote logical objects. This too is emphatically rejected by Wittgenstein in *TLP*, 4.0312: 'My fundamental idea is that the "logical constants" are not representives'; (German: nicht vertreten) 'that there can be no representatives of the *logic* of facts.'

$\phi$ and with $a$ does not involve any knowledge about them, but my acquaintance with $\xi$ x does involve the knowledge *that at least one other proposition of that form is true*, because the only way to achieve acquaintance with a form is to encounter an instance of it.

This is the vulnerable point that Wittgenstein must have attacked when the two philosophers met in May 1913. Russell, in his letter to Ottoline Morrell, reports that Wittgenstein said that he had tried Russell's theory and knew that it would not work. That is confirmed by an entry in the *Notebooks* dated 21 October 1914:

I used to think[7] that the possibility of the truth of the proposition $\phi$a was tied upwith the fact $(\exists$ x, $\phi).\phi$x. But it is impossible to see why $\phi$a should only be possible if there is another proposition of the same form [sc. another true proposition]. $\phi$a surely does not need any precedent. (For suppose that there existed only the two elementary propositions, '$\phi$a' and '$\psi$a' and that $\phi$a were false: Why should this proposition only make sense if '$\psi$a' is true?)   (*NB*, 21-x-14)

The divergence between Russell's theories of judgement and Wittgenstein's Picture Theory goes very deep. Russell believed that acquaintance, interpreted extensionally, was all that was needed in order to explain how sentences acquire their senses. Wittgenstein did not share that belief. In fact, he understates his case in this entry in the *Notebooks*. The trouble with Russell's 1913 theory of judgement is not only that there is no reason to suppose that the sense of one proposition depends on the truth of another.[8] Worse, if that really were so, there would be an infinite regress of propositions, each one owing its sense to the truth of the next one in the line. That would be a situation in which the sentential heavier-than-air machine could never get off the ground. This regress would run to infinity on a line parallel to the infinite regress that Wittgenstein used to prove that, if logical atomism were false, it would be impossible to construct any picture, true or false, of the world (see *TLP*, 2.0211–2.0212).

The Picture Theory avoids this disastrous outcome by making each sentence derive its sense independently from the segment of the world with which it is concerned:

---

[7] Anscombe's translation of 'Ich dachte' is 'I thought'. The point is that he no longer took the same view.

[8] This explains the way in which he formulates his criticism in his letter to Russell in June 1913. A correct theory of judgement must entail that the proposition that is judged true *already* has a sense, and it must entail this without the help of any other premisses.

One name stands for one thing, another for another thing, and they are combined with one another. In this way the whole group—like a tableau vivant—presents a state of affairs.   (*TLP*, 4.0311)

So the common feature of Russell's theory of meaning and Wittgenstein's Picture Theory is that both are Realist theories. For both treat the world as the dominant partner in the relationship with language which confers sense on its sentences. The difference between the two theories is that Wittgenstein offers a narrowly focused Realism, while Russell's Realism is, to say the least, diffuse.

The fate of the Picture Theory in Wittgenstein's later writings, is none too clear. The theory of meaning that he developed in the *Tractatus* was founded on two main doctrines, each supported by an argument from an infinite regress—the Picture Theory and Logical Atomism. Both theories were abandoned soon after he returned to philosophy in 1929, but there was a difference between the ways in which they were abandoned. Logical Atomism was explicitly rejected in 1929, [9] because it was impossible to see how elementary propositions could be logically independent of one another, but the Picture Theory simply faded out, apparently without receiving a mortal blow. It is true that there is some critical discussion of its details in the years immediately after Wittgenstein's resumption of philosophy in 1929, but nothing so devasting as his critique of Logical Atomism. So what is the explanation of the difference?

It is a plausible suggestion that the Picture Theory was outflanked by other developments in his philosophy and left to capitulate without any direct assault. If that is what happened, it is not too difficult to identify the new developments that produced this result. One is his realization that isolated ostensive definitions are never enough to fix the meanings of words; and the other is his rejection of the Realist explanation of the regular use of words.[10]

---

[9] In 'Some Remarks on Logical Form', *Proceedings of the Aristotelian Society*, Supplementary Vol., 1929; and *Philosophical Remarks*, Appendix 2, 'Yardstick and System of Propositions', 317.

[10] It is arguable that Wittgenstein's Picture Theory already contained the seeds of the ideas that led to its own supersession. For if a name stands for an object only so long as its combinations with other names conform to the possibilities of combination of its object with their objects, isolated ostensive definitions will always be inadequate. We shall always need two more pieces of information in order to grasp the meaning of a word. First, how are we to continue the line of applications of the word beyond the ostensive *definitions*?

The vulnerability of the Picture Theory to these two developments is evident. It is a theory based on the idea that a word derives its meaning from a single thing with which it is connected by a line like the line of projection that connects a point on a map with a point on the ground. It is also a theory that is overtly Realist in two distinct ways. First, the words in a sentence must be attached to objects; and, second, they must be combined only in ways that are possible for those objects. This is clearly a correspondence theory of sense, because in both these ways objects set the standard of fit and words bear the onus of fit.

The vulnerability of the Picture Theory to the critique of isolated ostensive definitions is a comparatively simple matter and it will be discussed in Chapter 3. Its vulnerability to the critique of Realism, which will be discussed in Chapter 2, is more complex. Is it really so obvious that the classical theories that seek to explain the meanings of general words—Realism and Nominalism—only offer empty explanations? Why, then, does their rejection seem so paradoxical? And why is Wittgenstein's appeal to incompletely formulatable linguistic techniques any better? It certainly sounds platitudinous, but, if so, what is its point?

This is the question that introduced Wittgenstein's discussion of linguistic regularity (see Ch. 2). Second, how will that line be affected by its intersections with the lines of application of other words? That is the question that led to the abandonment of Logical Atomism.

This is not to say that Wittgenstein's Picture Theory was not an example of Realism. The point is only that it was an uncritical Realism, which visibly contained the unsolved problems that would lead to its own supersession. This explains, but provides no real support for, Idealist interpretations of the ontology of the *Tractatus*.

# 2

## Linguistic Regularity

What holds together the things to which a general word applies and distinguishes them from other things? The idea behind Wittgenstein's treatment of linguistic regularity (commonly called 'rule-following')[1] is that the answers given to this question by traditional theories, like classical Realism and Nominalism, are empty because there is no independent way of identifying either the universals or the specific similarities that are invoked. Such theories are failed mimics of science and there is no place for them in philosophy, where

> ... we may not advance any kind of theory. There must not be anything hypothetical in our considerations. We must do away with all *explanation*, and description alone must take its place. And this description gets its light, that is to say its purpose from the philosophical problems.     (*PI* I, S 109, quoted at greater length above, p. ix.)

This does not mean that there are no ways of explaining the extensions of our general words and, in fact, there are often perfectly good scientific explanations of them. For example, the extensions of our colour-words may be explained by the physiology of our colour-vision, which, unlike the colour-vision of dogs, is sensitive to chromatic differences. Or the explanation might cite our interest in special features of our environment. But these would be scientific explanations and they would appeal to things that are identifiable independently of what they are required to explain. Philosophical explanations do not pass that test. That is a negative point and it can be applied to the question about the extensions of general words: genuine explanations of them will always be scientific. The point is made with great force and clarity in *PI* I, S 109.

But what, if anything, does philosophy have to say about linguistic regularity? We expect Wittgenstein's answer to be pithy and memorable, like the traditional answers that he rejects, Realism and Nominalism.

---

[1] But there need not be a formulated rule.

But it turns out to be very difficult to say exactly what his answer is. So different commentators pick different features of his treatment and optimistically treat them as central.

However, there is one line of investigation that might lead to a central point. He often describes the way in which someone can be taught the meaning of a word and the various ways in which he may misunderstand the lesson (for example, *PI*, SS 143 ff.). It is a conspicuous feature of these case-histories that the misunderstandings are often wildly improbable, and we may wonder why this is so. Evidently, the reason cannot be that Wittgenstein believed that such extreme misunderstandings are at all likely or that a teacher would need to guard against them in real life. So what is the explanation of his preoccupation with improbable misunderstandings? The answer to this question might put us on the road to grasping his central point about linguistic regularity.

The first step towards answering it was taken by Saul Kripke in his brilliant monograph, *Wittgenstein on Rules and Private Language* (Oxford, 1982). It is that Wittgenstein's point is not that such misunderstandings are probable, but only that they are possible. They are possible because, if the lesson only proceeds by examples, there will always be many different specifications of the meaning of the word that are satisfied by any finite sequence of examples, and so the pupil can always pick a specification that was not intended by the teacher. However, if the lesson has been well designed with carefully chosen examples, there will be only one *natural* way of interpreting them—or perhaps there will be minor variations, to be excluded easily by further examples. If, on the other hand, the teacher tries to close a gap by offering a definition of a problematic word, the words used in the definition will present the same problem again. Definitions, without the actual applications of the words that they contain, will merely lead to an infinite regress.

This was our paradox: no course of action could be determined by a rule, because every course of action can be made out to accord with the rule. The answer was: if everything can be made out to accord with the rule, then it can also be made out to conflict with it. And so there would be neither accord nor conflict here.

It can be seen that there is a misunderstanding here from the mere fact that in the course of our argument we give one interpretation after another; as if each one contented us at least for a moment, until we thought of yet another standing behind it. What this shows is that there is a way of grasping a rule which is *not* an *interpretation*, but which is exhibited in what we call 'obeying the rule' and 'going against it' in actual cases.    (*PI* I, S 201)

It is now generally agreed that this is not a sceptical demonstration of the impossibility, or even the improbability of successful instruction by examples. Wittgenstein's point is only that, when such lessons do succeed, as they often do in real life, they draw on a resource that is presupposed by the verbal interpretations and definitions but not mentioned in them. The extra resource, to put it at first quite generally and vaguely, is human nature.

The indispensable contribution made by human nature is described in an important text in C. Diamond (ed.), *Lectures on the Foundations of Mathematics* (Harvester, 1975):

First of all, to put the matter badly and in a way that must be corrected later, it is clear that we judge what a person means in these two ways. One can say that we judge what a person means by a word from the way he uses it. And the way he uses it is something that goes on in time. On the other hand, we also say that the meaning of a word is defined by the thing it stands for: it is something in our minds or at which we can point.

The connection between these two criteria is that the picture in our minds is connected, in an overwhelming number of cases—for the overwhelming majority of human beings—with a particular use. For instance, you say to someone 'This is red' (pointing); then you tell him 'Fetch me a red book'—and he will behave in a particular way. This is an immensely important fact about us human beings. And it goes together with all sorts of other facts of equal importance, like the fact that in all the languages we know, the meanings of words don't change with the days of the week.

Another such fact is that pointing is used and understood in a particular way—that people react to it in a particular way.

If you have learned a technique of language, and I point to this coat and, say to you, 'The tailors now call this colour "Boo" ', then you will buy me a coat of this colour, fetch one, etc. The point is that one only has to point at something and say 'This is so-and-so', and everyone who has been through a certain preliminary training will react in the same way. We could imagine this not to happen. If I just say, 'This is called "Boo" ', you might not know what I mean but in fact you would all of you follow certain rules. [*LFM*, 182]

If this reliance on what comes naturally to us is so important, it may seem surprising that Wittgenstein does not mention it more often. But that is probably because he always saw a clear difference between philosophy and the sciences (cf. *TLP*, 4.111 ff.). Indeed, it was the failure to appreciate the difference that caused the deep misunderstanding which was the main target of his critical thinking. Philosophy is so far from being another science that it does not seek any kind of explanation of the ways in which we think and speak. It takes them as given and it describes them, but it cannot explain them because it has no access to a deeper level of reality inaccessible to the sciences. So it cannot do what they can do: it cannot explain one thing by pointing to another, independently identifiable, thing.

That does not mean that there are no genuine explanations of the ways in which we think and speak. It only means that they cannot be achieved by philosophy. There is nothing wrong with the general thesis that we impose regularities on our own thoughts in order to discover regularities in the behaviour of things in our environment. Nor is there anything wrong with the general thesis that the need to communicate with other people and with one's own past self is a force that imposes standardization on natural languages. These are evidently the two main points of origin of linguistic normativity. Similarly, there is nothing wrong with the attempt to specify the relative advantages of the colour-vocabularies of different languages. Those would all be genuine scientific explanations because they would connect one thing with another, independently identifiable, thing and Wittgenstein's point is only that they would not belong to philosophy but to science.

If the formation of concepts can be explained by facts of nature, should we not be interested, not in grammar, but rather in that in nature which is the basis of grammar?—Our interest certainly includes the correspondence between concepts and very general facts of nature. (Such facts as mostly do not strike us because of their generality.) But our interest does not fall back upon these possible causes of the formation of concepts; we are not doing natural science; nor yet natural history.... (*PI* II, xii)

His programme is not easy to describe. On the one hand, philosophy does not explore a world of its own, like the physical world explored by the sciences but somehow lying behind it. If it did that, it would have to provide independent identifications of the things in the transcendent world that were supposed to explain the phenomena, but that is something that it cannot do. What it is able to do is to specify the conditions that make our thought and language possible but that can only be done scientifically on the phenomenal level. However, the point of doing it is not that it enables us to understand an ordinary phenomenal item—rather, it enables us to understand our own thought and language, and they constitute the lens through which we apprehend all phenomena, including the lens itself.

In *Lectures on the Foundations of Mathematics*, when he has distinguished between the natural continuation of the use of the new colour-word 'Boo' and unnatural continuations, he says:

This hangs together with the question of how to continue the series of cardinal numbers. Is there a criterion for the continuation—for a right and a wrong way—except that we do in fact continue them in that way, apart from a few cranks who can be neglected?    (*LFM*, 183; cf. *Remarks on the Foundations of Mathematics*, 3rd edn. I, s. 4)

He goes on to explain that the confidence with which we ignore the cranks is not based on our *opinion* that they are wrong, but on a consensus of *action*. This consensus is not something that can be assessed for truth or falsehood. It is, rather, a pre-condition of any assessment for truth or falsehood.

This has often been said before. And it has often been put in the form of an assertion that the truths of logic are determined by a consensus of opinions. Is this what I am saying? No. There is no *opinion* at all; it is not a question of *opinion*. They are determined by a consensus of *action*: a consensus of doing the same thing, reacting in the same way.   (*LFM*, 183–4)

Here he is making the point about the 'truths' of logic, but the context shows that he is extending it from its home ground, which is the meanings of individual words.

When he is developing this point, he stitches into his argument an inconspicuous parenthesis that will play a big role in his treatment of the same point in *Philosophical Investigations* I, SS 198–202:

Suppose someone said, 'Surely the use I make of the rule for continuing the series' [sc. of cardinal numbers] 'depends on the interpretation I make of the rule or the meaning I give it.' But is one's criterion for meaning a certain thing by the rule the using of the rule in a certain way, or is it a picture or another rule or something of the sort? In that case it is still a symbol—which can be reinterpreted in any way whatsoever.  (*LFM*, 183)

This topic is developed in *PI*, SS 198–202. It is obvious that, if someone is asked to explain the meaning of a word, he will have to use more words, as dictionaries do. However, nobody is worried by the use of language to explain non-linguistic matters, and we do not find fault with a cookery book because it contains only recipes. So why should we complain when a philosophical text contains nothing but verbal analyses of the meanings of words?

We might fail to be reassured by this answer because there is a fundamental difference between the two cases. If we want to know how to follow the recipes in a cookery book, we can ask someone to describe the requisite techniques and we would not complain that all that he gave us was more words. We would be content to hear the techniques described, because we would already know the meanings of the words used in their descriptions. We could, of course, ask for a demonstration, but we would not necessarily feel that the lesson was incomplete without one. But we might well complain if a philosophical text contained nothing but verbal analyses of the meanings of words. We might point out that it omitted an essential part of any theory of meaning: it told us a lot about the connections between words and other words, but nothing about the connections between words and the things to which we apply them—nothing about the interface between language and the world.

The short answer to this is that, if we want to be told, rather than shown, what happens at that interface, we can only be given more words. But there is a distinction to be drawn at this point: what we are asking for may not be the continuation of the analyses of particular words: it may be a general account of the application of words to things.

This general account is what Wittgenstein offers in his treatment of linguistic regularity in *Philosophical Investigations*. In the much-discussed passage running from S 198 to S 202, he argues that theories of meaning that merely offer verbal analyses of particular words leave the whole canopy of language 'hanging in the air', unattached to anything in our lives [*PI* I, S 198 and S 201). The remedy is to tie it down, and that is done in real life by actually applying words to things and in philosophy by giving a general account of the practice of applying words to things.

This part of *Philosophical Investigations* is an implicit criticism of the programme of the Vienna Circle and of the propositions of the *Tractatus* that had inspired it:

A name cannot be dissected any further by means of a definition: it is a primitive sign.

Every sign that has a definition signifies *via* the signs that serve to define it; and the definitions point the way.   (*TLP*, 3.26–3.261)

The logical atomism of the *Tractatus* had long been abandoned and what he is criticizing in *Philosophical Investigations*, SS 198–202, is preoccupation with definitions and the idea that, when they are no longer available, because the philosopher has reached words that are indefinable, all that he can do is to invoke the doctrine of showing, and say that an elementary proposition shows its sense (*TLP*, 4.1211). In fact, that is not his only resource: he can also give a general description of what happens at the interface between language and the world in a way that will make it intelligible, and the description can be realistic instead of being driven by the dogmatic assumptions of the *Tractatus*.

This was our paradox: no course of action could be determined by a rule, because every course of action can be made out to accord with the rule. The answer was: if everything can be made out to accord with the rule, then it can also be made out to conflict with it. And so there would be neither accord nor conflict here.

It can be seen that there is a misunderstanding here from the mere fact that in the course of our argument we give one interpretation after another; as if each one contented us at least for a moment, until we thought of yet another standing behind it. What this shows is that there is a way of grasping a rule which is *not* an *interpretation*, but which is exhibited in what we call 'obeying the rule' and 'going against it' in actual cases. (*PI* I, S 201)

But what *do* we call 'obeying a rule' and 'going against it'? Our answer to this question must not exaggerate the fixity of the meanings of words. They obviously change over time and any philosophical account of linguistic regularity has to allow for that fact. To use Wittgenstein's analogy, the beginning of a series of applications of a word may be like a 'visible section of rails' (*PI* I, S 218), but it would be rash to suppose that they are simply projected unchanged into the infinite future. We have to allow for the vitality and plasticity of language, and absolute linguistic regularity only extends over limited periods of time. Dictionaries mark the mutations by identifying two words where there had been only one before. During a period of average regularity there may be changes, but they must not be so rapid or so extreme that communication between contemporaries breaks down or the recovery of one's own past experiences, preserved in verbal memories, requires scholarship. In short, the changes must be natural and gradual.

Wittgenstein's abandonment of Platonic fixity of meaning is not too difficult to accept and the sticking-point for most commentators is the elusiveness of the alternative that he offers in *Philosophical Investigations*. The alternative is the suggestion that linguistic techniques are the ultimate repositories of meaning. We might object that in that case they cannot be quite as fluid as his account seems to allow. But what exactly does it allow? The best way to get an answer to this question is to see how far he has moved away from the pictorial theory of meaning of the *Tractatus*.

An idea like Wittgenstein's new idea had been formulated by the Greek philosopher Protagoras, who held that 'man is the measure of all things'. That would not be shocking if it meant that we use language in the same way that we use rulers, and that the criteria for the application of words were as objective as the coincidence of the length of an object with the distance between two lines on a ruler. But, of course, it means something much more paradoxical; it means that man himself is both measurer and measuring instrument. His reactions have taken over the role of the graduating lines on the ruler and they themselves serve as criteria for the application of his words. That is a truly minimalist doctrine.

The idea that man is the measure of all things in this second, more radical, sense, is the key to understanding Wittgenstein's later treatment of meaning. In the *Tractatus* he had argued that a sentence is a picture.

> 2.151 Pictorial form is the possibility that things are related to one another in the same way as the elements of the picture.
> 2.1511 *That* is how a picture is attached to reality: it reaches right out to it.
> 2.1512 It is laid against reality like a ruler.
> 2.15121 Only the end-points of the graduating lines actually *touch* the object to be measured.

This contact is the relation between name and object and the leading idea of the Picture Theory was that it automatically confers a definite sense on a sentence without any further contribution from the speakers who use it. Wittgenstein's later treatment of linguistic regularity is a rejection of this idea. The sense of a sentence is no longer completely determined by a single application of its words. We also need to know how the speaker will apply each word to other things. Isolated ostensive definitions are never enough to fix their meanings (*PI* I, SS 28–38). So we track his use of the words on other occasions, and, if anything is going to be like a ruler, it will be his usage rather than something that he uses—his technique rather than his instrument. He is the measure of all things in the radical sense of Protagoras' dictum.

However, disconcertingly, his techniques turn out to be very unlike rulers. Their criteria are often hard to pin down and it is sometimes impossible to formulate them in further words. In that case a speaker can only demonstrate his use of a word by actually applying it to things, and it is important that he can often do so so without the slightest hesitation. That is what Wittgenstein calls 'bedrock' [*PI* I, S 217]: there is no possibility of digging deeper and finding the kind of explanation of his technique that is offered in the *Tractatus*. Also, to make matters worse, the meanings of words are apt to change gradually but definitely over fairly long periods of time.

The much quoted passage from *Philosophical Investigations* (*PI* I, S 201: see above p. 23) is a *reductio ad absurdum* of the idea that a theory of meaning is like the theory of any other human activity and can be completely expressed in words. Its point is that such a theory of meaning would necessarily remain incomplete. Someone might suggest that we can complete it by adding descriptions of the techniques of applying words to things in the same way that we can add the descriptions of the culinary techniques that are taken for granted in a cookery book. But in the special case of language the deficiency can never be completely made good in that way, because what is lacking in this case is not the description of a technique but a demonstration of the technique itself. Language can be used to explain other human activities, but not—or, at least, not with the same non-controversial claim to completeness—itself.

Wittgenstein's own account of the difference between his early and his later treatment of meaning makes the situation very clear. His early idea had been that

we can hit upon something that we today cannot yet see, that we can *discover* something wholly new. That is a mistake. The truth of the matter is that we have already got everything and we have got it actually *present*: we need not wait for anything. We make our moves in the realm of the grammar of our ordinary language, and this grammar is already there. Thus we have already got everything and need not wait for the future. (*Ludwig Wittgenstein and the Vienna Circle*, B. McGuiness (ed.), (Blackwell, 1979), 182–3)

But though we have all the material that we need, it is not at all clear how we should use it in our account of linguistic regularity. Conversely, the *Tractatus* had told us exactly how to use material that we did not have.

These generalities need to be focused onto the concept of a linguistic technique. Suppose that Wittgenstein is right in thinking that the technique of using a general word can neither be frozen onto a universal nor completely captured in any verbal formulation. How, then, can it give us any guidance when we encounter a new thing and have to decide whether the word does or does not apply to it? To put the question in Lewis Carroll's terms: how does Wittgenstein's concept of a linguistic technique allow for any difference between Humpty-Dumpty's caprice ('It's my word and I can do what I like with it') and a conscientious attempt to apply the word correctly?

We may approach this question by way of a familiar paradox. If I really have no idea which specification of the series of things to which I have already applied a word ought to be projected into the future, then I do not know what meaning the word will have the next time I use it. I shall know a little more about the answer to that question only when I have encountered the next thing and decided whether or not the word is applicable to it. So the meaning is dependent on an ongoing investigation of my future reactions: will I or won't I apply the word to the next problematic thing? But if the investigation is formulated in this way, it is unintelligible. For if the word does not take its past meaning with it into the future, the question whether or not it applies to the next thing will not have a definite answer. If this paradox is validly constructed, how could Humpty-Dumpty even know when he was innovating? The very distinction between continuing a practice and modifying it seems to have collapsed, and we seem to be reduced to using a concept of linguistic regularity with as little force as a rubber sword. The only answer to the question 'does the word apply to this thing or not?' will be 'It applies if I apply it.' That would be Humpty-Dumpty's answer, and it would eliminate the very ideas of judgement and truth.

This is the 'paradox of investigation-dependence' and it is clearly unacceptable. But perhaps it is possible to use the concept of 'fit' to dismantle it. When a word is applied to a thing, it looks as if there ought to be only two possibilities. One is that the word has to fit the thing and, if it does fit it, the speaker's statement will be true. The other possibility is that the word acquires from the thing the standard of fit that will be imposed on it in its subsequent encounters with things. This is what happens when a thing is used to define the meaning of a word ostensively. Evidently, a single application of a word cannot combine these two functions in a simple, unqualified way. For there is a general requirement, that the meaning of a word must be fixed before there is any question of truth, and so the direction of fit must either be from word to thing or from thing to word. If there is no special qualification, it cannot run in both directions simultaneously. This is the point that is exploited by the paradox.

Plainly, an outright rejection of this point would be absurd, but it might be possible to qualify it by finding some special feature of the relation between language and world. Or, at least, the search might take us to the deeper point of Wittgenstein's reliance on linguistic techniques that can be effective without being finally and completely specified.

Consider the difference between material objects and techniques. If you are given a box of assorted nuts and bolts you can be handed a nut and asked to find a bolt that fits it, or you can be handed a bolt and asked to find a nut that fits it. The difference between these two tasks can be used to illustrate the difference between fitting a thing to a word in order to give the word a meaning and fitting a word to a thing in order to achieve truth.

However, the difference between fitting a word to a thing in order to achieve truth and fitting a thing to a word in order to give it a meaning is not exactly like the difference between the two ways of pairing assorted nuts and bolts. For when you are given a nut or a bolt your task is completely determined and in your search for its counterpart you can only use a single direction of fit. But when you are shown a thing and asked to find a word that fits it, you may have to innovate and stretch the meaning of the word that you suggest, but it does not follow that you will not be making a true statement or that it will be impossible for your audience to derive information about the thing from what you say. So the two directions of fit, which are rigidly exclusive in the case of nuts and bolts, are not quite so rigidly exclusive in the case of words and things. This leaves out the possibility that the hearer will immediately see the point of a linguistic innovation that may later become canonical and so he will be able to learn a truth about the thing to which the word is being applied. In such a case the innovation is ovoviviparous, like the method of reproduction used by certain snakes: the shift in the application of the word is no sooner inaugurated—that is the laying of the egg—than actually applied to record a truth—that is the immediate hatching of the egg.

Saul Kripke's monograph started the line of interpretation that has been continued in this chapter. So it might be useful to high-light the points where this continuation differs from his treatment. As many commentators have pointed out, Wittgenstein's argument in *Philosophical Investigations* I, S 201 is not that the relation between language and the world in itself presents a paradox, but only that it presents a paradox when it is interpreted in a certain way. The interpretation that is the culprit starts from the obvious need for a strong connection between something now in my mind when I apply the word and my future applications of it. Wittgenstein dismisses the possibility that this might be an a priori connection (*PI* I, S 201), and he goes on to reject the obvious alternative, that the present application of a word uses the same general formula as past applications of it. For past applications satisfy an infinite number of general formulas.

Kripke seems to take Wittgenstein's implication to be that the relation between language and the world is irremediably precarious. The argument of this chapter has been that it looks precarious only when we omit, as Kripke does, the essential contribution to linguistic regularity that is made by our common human nature. I have tried to show that this contribution is the central pillar of Wittgenstein's philosophy of language. But this is not easy to prove, because there are two things that make us overlook it. One is that its operation is hidden behind the more obvious pressure to conform to the linguistic community's requirement that we should agree in our judgements (*PI* I, SS 241–2). But that pressure would never have produced conformity without a common human nature to support it. The other thing that makes it difficult to prove the point is that any detailed argument for it would take us out of philosophy and into science. But why not?

It may be objected that human nature is shown in what people do and cannot, therefore, be used to explain what people do. Like the universals of classical Realism and the similarities of Nominalism, it fails to qualify as an independently identifiable factor. This is a valid objection, but what it shows is not that the general appeal to human nature is misguided, but only that it must be followed by a detailed account of our endowment and needs that will explain why we sort things in the ways that we do. This, of course, raises the question whether there really is a clear line of demarcation between this part of philosophy and science (cf. *PI* II, S xii).

Not surprisingly, Wittgenstein does not explore this frontier. But he does make two more important contributions to this topic, both well within the bounds of philosophy as he conceived it in his later writings. First, he gives a minimalist account of what it feels like to continue the regular application of a word. Then he asks what induces us to embellish this account by adding to it the picture of an irresistible external force exerted by something completely independent of our nature. His answer to this question is complex, and it will need to be analysed carefully. It is that we treat the contents of our own minds as symbols of their own future development. But what does that mean? That is not going to be an easy question to answer.[2]

The minimalist account is given succinctly in *Philosophical Investigations I*, S 219:

'All the steps are really already taken' means: I no longer have any choice. The rule, once stamped with a particular meaning, traces the lines along which it is to be followed through the whole of space.—But if something of this sort really were the case, how would it help?

---

[2] See below, pp. 30 ff.

No: my description only made sense if it was to be understood symbolically.—I should have said: *This is how it strikes me.*

When I obey a rule, I do not choose.

I obey the rule *blindly*.   (*PI* I, S 219)

Why blindly? Because the constraint comes from within—from our
own natures—and not from any external force, and so there is nothing
to be seen, and it is even questionable whether what we feel should
be called 'constraint'.[3] The idea that there are lines to be followed
through 'the whole of space' must be understood symbolically rather
than literally. It is only a dramatization of the experience of continuing
the application of a word, or of continuing the development of a
mathematical series.

S228 'We see a series in just *one* way!'—All right, but what is that way?
Clearly, we see it algebraically, and as a segment of an expansion. Or
is there more in it than that?—'But the way we see it surely gives us
everything!'—But that is not an observation about the segment of the
series; or about anything that we notice in it; it gives expression to the
fact that we look to the rule for instruction and *do something*, without
appealing to anything else for guidance.'

229 I believe that I perceive something drawn very fine in a segment of a
series, a characteristic design, which only needs the addition of 'and so
on' in order to reach to infinity.

230 'The line intimates to me which way I am to go' is only a paraphrase of:
it is my *last* arbiter for the way I am to go. (*PI* I, SS 228–30)

. . .

238 The rule can only seem to me to produce all its consequences in advance
if I draw them *as a matter of course*. As much as it is a matter of course
for me to call this colour 'blue' . . .   (ibid., *PI* I, S 238)

We externalize our feeling that something is a matter of course and it is
easy to see how this can generate one of the traditional theories, classical
Realism or Nominalism.

Wittgenstein also has another point to make about this externaliza-
tion, a point that is not so easy to understand. He uses an analogy to
make the point: the mind of a person who is about to develop a series
of regular uses of a word by applying it to yet another thing is like a
machine that is seen as a symbol of its own imminent action. This is
not a mechanistic theory of mind but only an analogy that he uses to
illustrate the origin of a philosophical illusion.

---

[3] Cf. *PI* I, S 140, discussed below, pp. 35–36.

The illusion is a misunderstanding of the experience of 'grasping the whole use of a word in a flash'. The misunderstanding has two causes. First, it feels to us as if the future applications of a word have already been made and are somehow stored in our minds for future use. Second, we treat what really is in the mind as a symbol of the mind's own future action, and so we conflate the two kinds of necessity, logical and nomological, and imagine that we can deduce this part of our future with a necessity that combines the strength of logical necessity with the informativeness of nomological necessity.

The first of the two illusions is analysed in *Philosophical Investigations* I, SS 187–8:

'But I already knew, at the time when I gave the order, that he ought to write 1002 after 1000.' Certainly; and you can also say that you *meant* it then; only you should not let yourself be misled by the grammar of the words 'know' and 'mean'. For you don't want to say that you thought of the step from 1,000 to 1,002 at that time—and even if you did think of this step, still you did not think of other ones. When you said 'I already knew at the time...' that meant something like: 'If I had then been asked what number should be written after 1,000 I should have replied "1002".' And that I don't doubt. This assumption is rather of the same kind as: 'If he had fallen into the water then, I should have jumped in after him.'—Now, what was wrong with your idea?     (*PI* I, S 187)

It is easy to see how this illusion works: We cannot cross a real bridge until we come to it,[4] but we can always substitute a notional bridge in our minds and imagine crossing it now. So we forget that the real problem about the development of a technique lies out of reach in the future.

The second illusion is more complex and more difficult to understand. How can a machine be taken as a symbol of its own future action? And how is that way of seeing a machine related to the conflation of the two kinds of necessity? And what has any of this to do with an illusion which generates a theory like Realism? The answers to these questions can be found in one of the most cryptic passages in *Philosophical Investigations*:

191 'It is as if we could grasp the whole use of the word in a flash.'—Like *what* e.g.?—Can't the use—in a certain sense—be grasped in a flash? And in *what* sense can it not?—The point is that it is as if we could 'grasp it in a flash' in yet another and much more direct sense than that.—But have you a model for this? No. It is just that this expression suggests itself to us. As the result of the crossing of different pictures.

---

[4] This platitude is used to illustrate a speaker's relation to his future application of a word in C.L. I, p. 67.

192 You have no model for this superlative fact, but you are seduced into using a super-expression. (It might be called a philosophical superlative.)

193 The machine as symbolizing its action: the action of a machine—I might say at first—seems to be there in it from the start. What does that mean?—If we know the machine, everything else, that is its movement, seems to be already completely determined.... (*PI* I, SS 191–3)

We need an example of a machine that can be used to illustrate the different ways in which we see its working. So picture a clock with its mechanism encased in glass so that the arrangement of its working parts is clearly visible. Then the question that we ask ourselves is 'what will it do when it has been wound and the mechanism starts working?'

Someone with an elementary knowledge of mechanics but no acquaintance with clocks or their function might predict the movement of the two hands on the face of the clock, and even their relative speeds and the points where they would coincide. The same predictions might be made by someone else who had no knowledge of mechanics but knew that the function of clocks is to tell the time and understood their language.

Now we might ask, 'Which of these two predictions is more likely to make us think that the future movement of the clock's hands is somehow already present and can be seen now without waiting for its actual occurrence?' Whichever it was, that prediction would treat what can be seen now as if it were related to the future development not as inductive evidence but, rather, as the record of a direct perception—somewhat like the crystal-gazing of a fortune-teller. So our question may be re-phrased like this: 'Which of the two predictions would treat the present state of the machine as a symbol of its future performance?'

The answer is that this treatment is not achieved by either of the two predictions when they are taken separately, but only when they are combined. The prediction based on the mechanical evidence treats the future development as something independent which would not happen if there were some fault in the mechanism. The prediction based on knowledge of the function of clocks simply assumes that this clock will not develop a fault and so will do what it was designed to do. When the two predictions are fused, we get the illusion that the future movement of its hands is guaranteed in a way that transcends all ordinary guarantees—it is guaranteed logically.

So Wittgenstein protests against the combination of two similar predictions made about a person who grasps the whole use of a word in a flash:

191 ... But have you a model for this? No. It's just that this expression suggests
    itself to us. As the result of the crossing of two different pictures.
192 You have no model for this superlative fact, but you are seduced into using
    a super-expression. (It might be called a philosophical superlative)    (*PI* I,
    SS 191–2).

A quick diagnosis of this misunderstanding would be that we treat the
future performance as if it were already actualized in the present state of
the person's mind, or in the present arrangement of the working parts of
the clock. Of course, nobody believes either of these two things because
it is too obviously always possible that something may go wrong, and,
even if all goes according to our expectations, the performance belongs
ineradicably to the future. But we are apt to be fooled by the vividness
of our own symbolism, which does everything possible to bring the
future forward into the present, without really meaning it. For example,
we often predict a future event by saying that it is going to happen. Or
in the blueprint of a machine we show the movement of the wheels by
small curved arrows. Or a fortune-teller says that she can actually see
the future catastrophe in her crystal.[5]

A general diagnosis of this misunderstanding would be that 'We
predicate of the thing what lies in our method of representing it' [*PI* I,
S 104]. For what misleads us in this case, as in so many others, is the
palpably false suggestion of our own symbolism. There is, therefore,
some truth in the idea that there must be something in us that wants
to be misled. George Orwell once asked, 'Has it ever struck you that
there's a thin man inside every fat man?—a thin man who, we may
suggest, wants to get out'—and something similar could be said about
language when it is driven by imagination but restrained by literalism.

This is the point of origin of Wittgenstein's therapeutic conception
of philosophy. Philosophical problems

... are, of course, not empirical problems; they are solved rather, by looking
into the workings of our language, and that in such a way as to make us
recognize those workings; *in despite of* an urge to misunderstand them. The
problems are solved, not by giving new information, but by arranging what
we have always known. Philosophy is a battle against the bewitchment of our
intelligence by means of language.   (*PI* I, S 109, quoted above, pp. ix and 17)

The culprit in this case is the combination of the two predictions
about the person who has grasped the meaning of a word in a flash.

---

[5] This way of thinking about the future seems to have distorted the New Wittgensteinians' account of the development of his philosophy. See above, p. 5 footnote 2.

There is nothing wrong in itself with the ordinary prediction, based on previous evidence, that he will continue to apply the word correctly. But, of course, it is a fallible prediction, because he may become confused and make mistakes, just as the mechanism of the clock may develop some fault. These are possibilities that can be discounted only if we switch to the other prediction, which is based on the known function of clocks. But there is a price to be paid for this strategy: if the clock malfunctions now, we shall conclude that it does not deserve to be called a clock. So we take it back to the shop where we bought it and say to the salesman 'This is no clock', and he replies, 'Then I suggest you find some other domestic use for it' (adaptation of a Monty Python joke). There is no third way of understanding the prediction—no way of achieving the absolute certainty of the second version without losing the informativeness of the first version. If you choose the benefit of logical necessity, you lose the benefit of nomological necessity.

This dilemma will be analysed in more detail in Chapter 4. It is the key to Wittgenstein's treatment of logical necessity. The point that needs to be made here is that any symbolic representation of the state of the world is apt to hide the price that we have to pay for absolute certainty of its future consequences. The working parts of a clock may bend or even melt, and if we insist that we are speaking about an ideal clock, we shall have to wait and see how this one performs before we concede that it really meets the standards of an ideal clock.

The point is explained in detail in *Lectures on the Foundations of Mathematics*:

If we talk of a logical machinery, we are using the idea of a machinery to explain a certain thing happening *in time*. When we think of a logical machinery explaining logical necessity, then we have a peculiar idea of the parts of the logical machinery—an idea which makes logical necessity much more necessary than other kinds of necessity. If we were comparing the logical machinery with the machinery of a watch, one might say that the logical machinery is made of parts which cannot be bent. They are made of infinitely hard material—and so one gets an infinitely hard necessity.

How can we justify this sort of idea?

------------------------------------------------------------------------

Perhaps it would help to take the example of a perfectly inexorable or infinitely hard law, which condemns a man to death.

A certain society condemns a man to death for a crime. But then a time comes when some judges condemn every person who has done so-and-so, but others let some go. One can then speak of an inexorable judge or a lenient judge. In a similar way, one may speak of an inexorable law or a lenient law, meaning that it fixes the penalty absolutely or it has loopholes. But one can also speak of an inexorable law in another sense. One may say that the law condemns him to death, whether or not the judges do so. And so one says that, even though the judge may be lenient, the law is always inexorable. Thus we have the idea of a kind of super-hardness.

-----------------------------------------------------------------------

In kinematics we talk of a connecting rod—not meaning a rod made of brass or steel or what-not. We use the word 'connecting rod' in ordinary life, but in kinematics we use it in quite a different way, although we say roughly the same things about it as we say about the real rod: that it goes forward and back, rotates, etc. But then the real rod contracts and expands, we say. What are we to say of this rod? Does it contract and expand?—And so we say it *can't*. But the truth is that there is no question of it contracting or expanding. It is a *picture* of a connecting rod, a symbol used in this symbolism for a connecting rod. And in this symbolism there is nothing which corresponds to a contraction or expansion of the connecting rod.

-----------------------------------------------------------------------

Similarly, if I say that there is no such thing as the super-rigidity of logic, the real point is to explain where this idea of super-rigidity comes from—to show that the idea of *super-rigidity* does *not* come from the same source which the idea of *rigidity* comes from. The idea of rigidity comes from comparing things like butter and elastic with things like iron and steel. But the idea of super-rigidity comes from the interference of two pictures—like the idea of the super-inexorability of the law. First we have: 'The law condemns', 'The judge condemns'. Then we are led by the parallel use of the pictures to a point where we are inclined to use a superlative. We have then to show the sources of this superlative, and that it doesn't come from the source the ordinary idea comes from.    (*LFM*, 196–9)

This line of reasoning is the key to Wittgenstein's analysis of logical necessity.[6] It is repeated in *Remarks on the Foundations of Mathematics* I, SS 118–24. When it is applied to the experience of grasping the meaning of a word in a flash, the point is that it is an illusion to suppose that I can achieve absolute certainty about my future applications of a word by relying on my present experience. Even if I have been thoroughly trained in its use, tomorrow's performance may still be faulty, and the absolute reliability of yesterday's inference can be salvaged only by saying that my training cannot really have been complete after all. There is another

-----

[6] See Ch. 4.

discussion of this illusion in *Philosophical Investigations* and it deals with a case where the application of a word is based on a mental image:

139  When someone says the word 'cube' to me, for example, I know what it means. But can the whole *use* of the word come before my mind, when I *understand* it in this way?

Well, but on the other hand isn't the meaning of the word also determined by this use? And can't these ways of determining meaning conflict? Can what we grasp *in a flash* accord with a use, fit or fail to fit it? And how can what is present to us in an instant, what comes before our mind in an instant, fit a *use*?

What really comes before our mind when we *understand* a word?—Isn't it something like a picture? Can't it *be* a picture?

Well, suppose that a picture does come before your mind when you hear the word 'cube', say the drawing of a cube. In what sense can this picture fit or fail to fit a use of the word 'cube'?—Perhaps you say, 'It's quite simple;—if that picture occurs to me and I point to a triangular prism for instance, and say it is a cube, then this use of the word doesn't fit the picture.'—But doesn't it fit? I have purposely so chosen the example that it is quite easy to imagine a *method of projection* according to which the picture does fit after all.

The picture of the cube did indeed *suggest* a certain use to us, but it was possible for me to use it differently.

140  Then what sort of mistake did I make; was it what we should like to express by saying, 'I should have thought the picture forced a particular use on me'? How could I think that? What *did* I think? Is there such a thing as a picture, or something like a picture, that forces a particular application on us; so that my mistake lay in confusing one picture with another?[7]—For we might be inclined to express ourselves like this: we are at most under a psychological, not a logical, compulsion.

And now it looks quite as if we knew of two kinds of case.     (*PI* I, SS 139–40)

The crucial question in this text is, 'Is there such a thing as a picture, or something like a picture, that forces a particular application on us?' Wittgenstein's adversary in this dialectical discussion has been suggesting

---

[7] This is an awkward translation. The German text only asks whether my mistake lay in a confusion. No doubt, the mistake would lie in confusing one picture with another and in S 191 and in *LFM*, 199 he does say that it would be the result of crossing two different pictures. But in this context, where what is being discussed is the way in which a picture in a person's mind might influence his application of a word, it is awkward to speak of two different pictures of its influence. No doubt, that is why the German only asks whether my mistake lay in a confusion rather than asking whether it lay in a confusion between one picture and another.

that there really is such a thing. If he were right, there would be a clear distinction between two possibilities: either my future use of the word 'cube' would fit the picture or it would fail to fit it, and it would be correct only if it did fit it. Consequently, if my training had succeeded in fixing the picture in my mind, there would be little doubt that my future use of the word would be correct.

But Wittgenstein rejects the idea that there could be any such meaning-fixer[8] in a person's mind. He points out that, even if he did get a mental picture of a cube, it would be compatible with different ways of continuing the application of the word 'cube'. To generalize his point, when the pupil has learned how to use the word, there is nothing in his mind to indicate that he can now graduate—not even something that God alone could see if He looked into his mind (cf. *PI* II, xi, p. 217).

Wittgenstein caps this point by undermining his adversary's idea that there are really two kinds of compulsion that might be operating in this case: one psychological; and the other logical. 'For we might be inclined to express ourselves like this: we are at most under a psychological, not a logical compulsion. And now it looks quite as if we knew of two kinds of case.' This is ironical because he did not believe that there is really any such thing as logical compulsion. Compulsion is imposed on a person by some external force, but he believed that so-called 'logical compulsion' is self-imposed.[9]

---

[8] What I called a 'magic talisman' in my book *The False Prison* (Oxford, 1988) ii. 209–10.

[9] See Ch. 4, for the development of his view that logical compulsion is self-imposed. In *RFM* I, 118, he introduces the discussion of the inexorability of laws and the super-rigidity of connecting rods by saying: 'It looked at first as if these considerations were meant to show that "what seems to be a logical compulsion is in reality a psychological one"—only here the question arose: am I acquainted with both kinds of compulsion then?!'

# 3

# The Private Language Argument

When Wittgenstein applied his account of linguistic regularity to the sensation-language, it generated the so-called 'Private Language Argument'. He did not use this name for the argument and it was coined by early readers of *Philosophical Investigations*. It can be a misleading name because it seems to imply that he employed a single knock-down argument against the possibility of a Private Language but, in fact, both the texts in which the argument is developed present a running battle against Private Language rather than a single engagement.[1] So the search for a single argument may well be the result of an over-simplification.

However, there is no doubt that both texts criticize the same idea, which is identified very clearly in *Philosophical Investigations*:

But could we also imagine a language in which a person could write down or give vocal expression to his inner experiences—his feelings, moods and the rest—for his private use?—Well, can't we do so in our ordinary language?—But that is not what I mean. The individual words of this language are to refer to what can only be known to the person speaking; to his immediate private sensations. So another person cannot understand the language.   (*PI* I, S 243)

This should be compared with his earlier specification of a 'Private Language' in the *Notes for Lectures*:

In fact, if he is to play a language-game, the possibility of this will depend upon his own and the other people's reactions. The game depends upon the agreement of these reactions; i.e. they must describe the same things as 'red'.

But if he speaks to himself, surely this is different. For then he needn't consult other people's reactions and he just gives the name 'red' now to the *same colour* to which he gave it on a previous occasion. But how does he know that it is *the same colour*? Does he also recognize the sameness of colour as what

---

[1] The two texts are 'Notes for Lectures on "Private Experience" and "Sense-data (1936)"' (published in *Philosophical Review*, 1977, and repr. in *Ludwig Wittgenstein, Philosophical Occasions 1912–1951*, ed. James Klagge and Alfred Nordmann (Hackett, 1993), and *Philosophical Investigations* I, SS 243 ff.

he used to call sameness of colour and so on ad inf[initum]? . . .   (*Notes for Lectures* in *Philosophical Occasions*, 1993, 234)

So the target of Wittgenstein's criticism was the idea that a person could describe his own sense-impressions (and, more generally, anything else 'within his mind') without relying in any way on their connections with anything in the physical world. If we really could do this, the 'world within the mind' would be completely self-sufficient. That would be a rash assumption, made conspiciously and with great panache by Berkeley in his *Three Dialogues*,[2] and it was still the dominant tradition when Wittgenstein was working out the consequences of his account of linguistic regularity. There is no doubt about the target of his critique, and its impact on its target will help to establish its general character. Then the controversial details can be filled in later.

The general character of his critique of 'Private Language' can be seen most clearly in the way in which he summed it up in his later references to it. In his *Notes for Philosophical Lecture*,[3] he writes:

The relation between name and object. Lang[uage] game of builders. What is the relation between names and actions, names and shapes? The relation of ostensibly [*sic*] defining. That's to say, in order to establish a name-relation we have to establish a technique of use. And we are misled if we think that it is a peculiar process of christening an object which makes a word a word for that object. This is a kind of superstition. So it's no use saying that we have a private object before the mind and give it a name. There is a name only where there is a technique of using it and that technique can be private; but this only means that nobody but I can know about it, in the sense that I can have a private sewing machine.[4] But in order to be a private sewing machine, it must be an object that deserves the name 'sewing machine', not in virtue of its privacy, but in virtue of its similarity to sewing machines, private or otherwise.   (*Philosophical Occasions*, p. 448)

The technique of using the name is essential, but if all that we had was an ostensive definition that attached the word to a private object, there would be no technique. The question is, 'why not?'

The same point is made by an analogy that he used in order to illustrate the effect of severing all connections between a supposed Private Language and everything in the physical world. If the engine

---

[2]  G. Berkeley, *Dialogues between Hylas and Philonomous*, (1713).

[3]  Intended as a lecture to the British Academy in 1941, but never given: now included in *Philosophical Occasions*, 1912–51, 445–58.

[4]  He made a sewing machine that worked when he was 13 years old.

of a motor-roller had a rigid piston mounted inside its drum, not only would it fail to produce any effect outside the drum (it would not make it roll) but also it would not be doing anything inside the drum (it too would not move) (*Philosophical Grammar*, S 141 and *Zettel*, S 248). In a third reference to this analogy (*Remarks on the Philosophy of Psychology* 1. S 317), he says that when he first thought of it, he did not appreciate the second deficiency: i.e., he saw that a language set up in isolation from the physical world could not be used to describe it, but he did not see that it would be equally incapable of describing the world within the mind because it would not be doing anything there either.

> The example of the motor-roller with the motor in the cylinder [i.e., in the drum] is actually far better and deeper than I have explained. For when someone showed me the construction, I saw at once that it could not function, since one could roll the cylinder [i.e. the drum] from outside even when the 'motor' was not running; but *this* I did not see, that it was a rigid construction and not a machine at all. And here there is a close analogy with the private ostensive definition. For here too, there is, so to speak, a direct and an indirect way of gaining insight into the impossibility.   (see *Zettel*, S 248; and *Remarks on the Philosophy of Psychology*, i. S 397)

He must mean that the indirect way would be to see that a language could never be set up without any connections with the physical world, and the direct way would be to see that the would-be speaker of such a language would not be doing anything that would count as practising a technique even within his mind. But both these insights need to be developed and explained in detail.

Before that task is undertaken, we need a more detailed identification of the target of Wittgenstein's critique. It is, of course, nothing less than the entire Cartesian picture of the relation between mind and body, but its specific target—as it were, the bull's-eye—was the account of perception and language current in the Vienna Circle and especially the account given by Carnap in *Der Logische Aufbau der Welt* (1928).[5] According to Carnap, our sensations are bracketed between stimuli and responses and each of us really speaks two languages: one specifying our sensations in physical terms based on the stimuli that produce them and on the responses that they, in their turn, produce, and the other specifying them in purely sensory terms. It is easy to understand how we communicate with one another in the first of these two languages,

---

[5] The English translation by R. A. George was published by Open Court in 2003 under the title *The Logical Structure of the World*.

but the second one would be private in the strong sense investigated by Wittgenstein.

This account of perception and language is criticized in *Philosophical Investigations* I, SS 272–3:

272 The essential thing about private experience is really not that each person possesses his own exemplar, but that nobody knows whether other people also have *this* or something else.

The assumption would thus be possible—though unverifiable—that one section of mankind had one sensation of red and another section another.

273 What am I to say about the word 'red'?—that it means something 'confronting us all', and that everyone should really have another word, besides this one, to mean his *own* sensation of red? . . .     (*PI* I, SS 272–3)

It is an important fact about the development of Wittgenstein's philosophy that in 1929 he was prepared to explore the possibility of interpreting the objects of the *Tractatus* as sense-data (see Merrill and Jakko Hintikka, *Investigating Wittgenstein*, ch. 2). So in *Philosophical Remarks* (1929–31) there is a more sympathetic treatment of the theory that is mocked in the passage just quoted from *Philosophical Investigations*.

We could adopt the following way of representing matters: if I, L.W. have toothache then that is expressed by means of the proposition 'There is toothache'. But if that is so, what we now express by the proposition 'A has toothache' is put as follows 'A is behaving as L. W. does when there is toothache'.[6] Similarly, we shall say 'It is thinking' and 'A is behaving as L. W. does when it is thinking'. . . . It's evident that this way of speaking is equivalent to ours when it comes to questions of intelligibility and freedom from ambiguity. But it's equally clear that this language could have anyone at all as its centre.     (*PR*, S 58)

This is followed by a discussion of some of the details of the theory about the two levels of language: one specifying sensations by the stimuli and responses that bracket them; while the other specifies them directly in purely sensory terms. The difficulty that threatens the theory is that there is nothing to guarantee the identity of a sensation of A's specified in B's indirect physical way with a sensation of A's specified in A's direct sensory way.

The difficulty was not new: it had been pointed out by Russell in 1917 (see Russell, *The Philosophy of Logical Atomism* in *Essays in Logic and*

---

[6] Note the absence of any mention of the stimulus: see below p. 43.

*Knowledge*, ed. R.C. Marsh, 1951). Russell accepted it as inevitable but, of course, it raises a further question: 'what then is the role of sensations when they are specified directly in sensory terms?' Wittgenstein's later answer to this question was that they have no role at all *if they are treated as independent inner objects*, and so, since they obviously do have a role, they must be treated in some other way.[7] In this earlier text he had not yet reached that point, because he had not yet formulated his argument against the possibility of a Private Language. It makes its first appearance in 1936 in *Notes for Lectures on 'Private Experience' and 'Sense-data'.*[8] Sensation-language is the main battleground but, naturally, if sensations stand in need of physical criteria, so too do all inner entities (cf. *PI*, S 580).

The best way to approach the 'Private Language Argument' is to follow the order of Wittgenstein's own exposition in *Philosophical Investigations* (a point first stressed by Saul Kripke in his *Wittgenstein on Rules and Private Language*, (Basil Blackwell, Oxford, 1982)). First, we must ask what resources are needed to preserve the regularity of our uses of words when we record the world around us; and then we must ask which of those resources would be lacking when we move on to the deceptively similar-looking task of recording the world within our minds after its contents have been isolated from the world around us. The outcome of this investigation, when it is conducted by Wittgenstein, is going to be that, if we treat sensations as independent objects with independent criteria of identity, as Carnap does in *Der Logische Aufbau der Welt*, then all our attempts to record them will implode and be reduced to nothing.

The general drift of Wittgenstein's critique of Private Language is much clearer than the details. His leading idea is that the language in which we report sensations owes its meaning to their connections with the physical world and cannot survive separation from it. This is presented very clearly in a passage in *Philosophical Remarks* in which he criticizes the sceptical thesis that what is given in perception is illusory and the reality beyond it unattainable:

What I wanted to say is it's strange that those who ascribe reality only to things and not to our ideas move about so unquestioningly in the world as idea and never long to escape from it.

In other words, how much a matter of course the given is. It would be the very devil if this were a tiny picture taken from an oblique, distorting angle.

[7] This answer is easily misunderstood as the unconditional assertion that they have no role at all. See *PI* I, S 304.

[8] See p. 37, n. 8.

This, which we take as a matter of course, *life*, [9] is supposed to be something accidental, subordinate; while something that normally never comes into my head, reality!

That is, what we neither can nor want to go beyond would not be the world.

Time and again the attempt is made to use language to limit the world and set it in relief—but it can't be done. The self-evidence of the world expresses itself in the very fact that language can and does only refer to it.

For since language only derives the way in which it means, its meaning, from the world, no language is conceivable that does not represent this world.   (*PR*, S 47)

This protest against the Cartesian detachment of the mental world from the physical world, which leads to a misrepresentative theory of perception, fixes the general drift of his critique of 'Private Language'. But the details are far less clear.

If we want to know why this is so, we must go back to the premiss of the 'Private Language Argument' and we must ask how Wittgenstein moved from his premiss to his conclusion that such a language would be impossible. His premiss was the thesis that to speak a language is to practise a technique, and that the technique is the ultimate repository of meaning. That was the outcome of his discussion of linguistic regularity. The question now is 'How did he deduce the impossibility of a Private Language from that premiss?'

The first step is to see that practising a technique is a case of acting intentionally. Now anyone who acts intentionally must know two things: he must know what he is engaged in doing; and he must know when he has succeeded in doing it. There are two main interpretations of the route followed by Wittgenstein in the 'Private Language Argument' and each of them is closely connected to one of the two things that anyone who is acting intentionally needs to know. The interpretation that was most widely adopted when *Philosophical Investigations* was first published (and was adopted in my book, *The False Prison*[10]) took the obstacle to a Private Language to be that the would-be speaker would never know if he was continuing to apply a word correctly. The interpretation recently proposed by Barry Stroud[11] suggests that the speaker would never know what he was engaged in doing, because his

---

[9] Cf. *TLP*, 5.621: 'The world and life are one.'

[10] See '*The False Prison*', ii. chs. 13–15.

[11] Barry Stroud, 'Private Objects, Physical Objects and Ostension', in David Charles and Bill Child (eds.), *Wittgensteinian Themes, Essays in Honour of David Pears* (Oxford, 2001). See below, pp. 45–46.

only resource would be an ostensive definition and an isolated ostensive definition is never enough to fix the meaning of a word.

These two interpretations are not exclusive rivals. For the would-be speaker of a Private Language who did not know what he was engaged in doing would also fail to know when he had succeeded in doing it. But the interesting case for the first interpretation is the case of someone who did know what he was engaged in doing but did not know when he had succeeded in doing it.

There is also another complication that affects the assessment of the two interpretations. In his development of the 'Private Language Argument' Wittgenstein uses examples of two very different kinds. One kind of example is an exteroceptive sense-impression, such as a visual impression of a colour. The other kind of example is the sensation of pain. A lot of attention is devoted to the first kind of example in the development of the 'Private Language Argument' in *Notes for Lectures*. In *Philosophical Investigations* the discussion covers both kinds of example, but is more concerned with the case of pain.

The interpretation of the 'Private Language Argument' that I defended in *The False Prison* focused on the first of these two kinds of example and was based on *PI* I, S 258–60:

S 258 Let us imagine the following case. I want to keep a diary about the recurrence of a certain sensation. To this end I associate it with the sign 'S' and write this sign in a calendar for every day on which I have the sensation.—I will remark first of all that a definition of the sign cannot be formulated.[12]—But still I can give myself a kind of ostensive definition.—How? Can I point to the sensation? Not in the ordinary sense. But I speak or write the sign down, and at the same time I concentrate my attention on the sensation—and so, as it were, point to it inwardly. But what is this ceremony for? For that is all it seems to be! A definition surely serves to establish the meaning of a sign.—Well, that is done precisely by the concentration of my attention, for in this way I impress on myself the connection between the sign and the sensation.—But 'I impress it on myself' can only mean that this process brings it about that I remember the connection *right* in the future. But in the present case I have no criterion of correctness. One would like to say: whatever is going to seem right to me is right. And that only means that here we cannot talk about 'right'!

[12] No verbal definition of 'S' is available and so its meaning can be given only by applying it to examples at the interface between language and the world, and, according to the theory under attack, they would always be sensory examples.

S 259  Are the rules of the private language *impressions* of rules?—The balance
on which impressions are weighed is not the *impression* of a balance.

S 260  'Well, I *believe* that this is the sensation S again.'—Perhaps you *believe*
that you believe it!...   (*PI* I, SS 258–60)

This criticism would undermine the attempt to introduce a colour-
vocabulary solely by its application to impressions of the different
colours.[13] The point would be that a colour-word like 'blue' could not
be given a stable meaning by a would-be private linguist, whose only
resource would be his visual impressions of blue without any regular
connections with blue physical objects. He would have to rely on the
remembered similarity of a sequence of visual impressions. That was
exactly what he was required to do in the 'original position' described
by Carnap.[14] Wittgenstein's criticism is that this would not be a reliable
basis for linguistic regularity. The only way to get a reliable basis would
be to use physical objects independently known to be blue, as we do
when we test a person for colour-blindness.

Some difficulty might be felt about Wittgenstein's complaint that in
such a case there would be no criterion of correctness. For that suggests
that it is truth, rather than meaning, that is in question. But learning
the meaning of a word is learning to make true statements with it
and this pupil's failure to make true statements would show that he
had not acquired the technique of applying it, and, therefore, had not
learned its meaning. If he were colour-blind, he could not acquire the
technique.

Another difficulty that might be felt about this interpretation of
the 'Private Language Argument' is that it seems to make it rely on
the assumption that correct recognition of a colour is easier and more
reliable than correct recognition of an impression of a colour. But is that
really so? Philosophers who reject the argument say, 'I am sure that I
could recognize my sense-impressions even if they were not connected in
any way with the physical world.' Maybe so. But that is because they are
imagining themselves already trained in this world to use a vocabulary
for exteroceptive perceptual impressions and taking it with them into
another world, where there would be no established connections between
sense-impressions and physical objects. But can they also imagine living
*their whole lives* in the world that lacked these connections and still

---

[13] Cf. *Notes for Lectures*, in *Philosophical Occasions, 1912–1951*, p. 234, where the
point is applied to impressions of colour.

[14] Carnap, 'The Logical Structure of the World', p. 98 ff.

setting up a language for reporting their sense-impressions? That really would be a way of challenging Wittgenstein's argument.

Barry Stroud has recently objected to this interpretation of the 'Private Language Argument' and suggested an alternative interpretation (see above, p. 42). His objection is that the proposed interpretation commits Wittgenstein to a version of foundationalism as objectionable as the version that he rejects. According to him, if Wittgenstein's criticism of Private Language is interpreted in this way, it makes a mistake exactly like the mistake that it imputes to the hypothesis that it attacks. For both the hypothesis and the criticism are examples of an untenable foundationalism. The hypothesis treats reports of sensations as the independent foundations of all other contingent statements, while the criticism simply transfers this treatment to statements about physical objects.

But this is a misunderstanding of Wittgenstein's position. It is true that he rejects the idea that reports of sensations should be treated as the independent foundation of the whole edifice of empirical knowledge. But he does not simply transfer that treatment to statements about physical objects. This controversy is not like a see-saw with a simple mechanism that can bring down one of the two opposed theories only by elevating the other to the same pretentious height. There is also a third possibility: the two kinds of statement may form an interlocking system to which each makes its own specific contribution. That seems to have been Wittgenstein's view.[15]

Stroud's alternative interpretation of *PI* I, S 258 is that the would-be private linguist's only resource is ostensive definition, but that would not enable him to set up a language for reporting his sensations, because ostensive definitions are inscrutable. The word 'S' in S 258 is supposed to be defined by its attachment to a particular sensation, but the attachment will not be enough in itself to determine what aspect of the sensation is going to be the basis of further applications of the word. More is needed if the ostensive definition is going to establish a technique. Essentially the same point had been made in the eighteenth century by Berkeley and Hume in their discussions of general ideas: the idea of *blue* occurs in the mind as a particular image, but because it cannot resemble every shade of blue, it achieves its general representation by standing in for all the shades including its own, like a hieroglyph. Somewhat similarly,

[15] Cf. 'The world and life are one' (*TLP*, 5. 621) and the more detailed development of this balanced theory in *PR*, S 47, quoted above, pp. 41–42.

Wittgenstein would say that the generality of the word consists in the use that we make of it.[16]

There is no doubt that the inscrutability of isolated ostensive definitions plays a role in Wittgenstein's critique of Private Language. It occupies a prominent position not only in *PI* I, S 258 but also in the remarks that precede it and follow it. In S 257 he says,

And when we speak of someone's having given a name to pain, what is presupposed is the existence of the grammar of the word 'pain'; it shows the post where the new word is stationed.    (*PI* I, S 257)

And in *PI* I, S 261 he asks

What reason have we for calling 'S' the sign for a *sensation*? For 'sensation' is a word of our common language, not of one intelligible to me alone. So the use of this word stands in need of a justification which everybody understands.—And it would not help either to say that it need not be a *sensation*, that when he writes 'S', he has *something*—and that is all that can be said. 'Has' and 'something' also belong to our common language.—So in the end, when one is doing philosophy one gets to the point where one would just like to emit an inarticulate sound—But such a sound is an expression only as it occurs in a particular language-game, which should now be described.    (*PI* I, S 261)

The inscrutability of isolated ostensive definitions is discussed in a general way in *PI* I, SS 28–32, and it is used as an objection to the hypothesis of a Private Language in the remarks quoted above. The objection is also given a prominent position in the *Notes for a Philosophical Lecture* in which Wittgenstein reviews the case against a *Private Language* (*Philosophical Occasions 1912–1951*, ed. Klagge and Nordmann, 448, quoted above, p. 38).

But though there is no doubt that he used the inscrutability of isolated ostensive definitions as an objection to the Private Language hypothesis, it is not at all clear what the force of the objection is. The general idea is clear enough: a single, exemplary application of a word is not enough to fix the way in which the technique of applying it is to be developed. But why should the would-be private linguist be restricted to a single application of the word? It is true that Wittgenstein puts into his mouth an appeal to an isolated ostensive definition of 'S' (*PI*

---

[16] Cf. *LFM*, 182, quoted above, p. 19: '... you say to someone "This is red" (pointing): then you tell him "Fetch me a red book"—and he will behave in a particular way. This is an immensely important fact about us human beings, and it goes together with all sorts of other facts of equal importance like the fact that in all the languages we know the meanings of words don't change with the days of the week.'

I, S 258) and that certainly imputes a mistake to him. But why should he make this mistake? What is there to prevent him from saying 'The ostensive definition is only the first step in fixing the meaning of "S". It is not complete in itself and it needs to be supplemented by my further applications of the word'? That is what he would say if he coined a new word in a public language. So what stops him saying it about a new word in his private language? If a criticism of the Private Language hypothesis is going to be based on the inscrutability of isolated ostensive definitions, this question must be answered. There ought to be some special feature of an ostensive definition of a word in a Private Language that blocks this move. But what could it be?

It is an important feature of Wittgenstein's critique that he simply puts the appeal to isolated ostensive definitions into the mouth of the would-be private linguist without more ado. This is a legitimate ascription if the hypothesis of a Private Language is grafted onto the theory of language developed in the *Tractatus*, where names were given meanings by isolated ostensive definitions. Carnap, too, in *The Logical Structure of the World*, gives names their meanings by isolated attachment to their objects.[17] But there was no need for the isolation and it was a great improvement to add the later expansion of the technique of applying a word, and so to give its meaning a broader basis. But the failure to add this improvement has no necessary connection with privacy. So perhaps Wittgenstein's criticism was quite generally focused onto any theory of meaning that relied on isolated ostensive definitions. If so, it would have its targets, but they would have no special connection with privacy. If it is going to be connected with privacy, there must be a reason for putting the appeal to isolated ostensive definitions into the mouth of the would-be private linguist.

However, it is not at all clear what the reason could be. It is obvious that the shorter the sequence of applications of a word the greater the scope for misunderstanding its meaning, and a single application is the limiting case, with maximal scope for misunderstanding. But that is just as true of an application of a word to a physical object as it is of an application to a sense-impression. So, as far as this point goes, Carnap's pioneer in the original position is no worse off than the average person in the physical world. Both confront a situation in which a reasonably long sequence of applications of a word is not only desirable but also possible. It is, therefore, not clear why Wittgenstein would load the dice

---

17 See *The Logical Structure of the World*, 98–136.

against the would-be private linguist by committing him to belief in the efficacy of isolated ostensive definitions. Perhaps this feature of his critique is only *ad hominem*: for in the *Tractatus* he himself had relied on isolated ostensive definitions, and so, too, had Carnap in *The Logical Structure of the World*. These are important historical facts, but they do not affect the concept of a private language.

There is another, connected element in his critique which raises a similar problem of interpretation. He mentions several times that, when a word is introduced in a language, there must already be a place for it. In *PI* I,S 257 and S 261 (quoted above, p. 46) he argues that it would be impossible for the would-be private linguist to introduce names for sensations unless there were already a place in his language prepared for them and waiting to be occupied by them. For example, the word 'pain' is the name of a type of sensation that is not exteroceptive, and is associated with certain kinds of behaviour. So it cannot be introduced by simple attachment to a sensation but must be assigned to the correct position in a complex holistic system.

This objection to a Private Language is related to the preceding objection in an interesting way. The point made by the critique of isolated ostensive definitions was that it is a mistake to try to base the meaning of a word on a single application, and the rejection of that mistake was the starting-point of Wittgenstein's long investigation of linguistic regularity. The point made by this objection is that it is a mistake to try to introduce a word for a specific sensation, like pain, before fixing its place in language (it is a sensation but not exteroceptive (cf. *PI* I, S 312)) and before fixing its place in daily life (it signals damage and, wherever possible, leads to avoiding action and it is an appeal for sympathy and help (cf. *Zettel*, SS 537–43)). Both objections appeal to holistic features—features of the language in the first case and, in the second case, features of the situation in which the word is introduced into the language.

The answer proposed to the first of these two objections was that there is no need for the would-be private linguist to start from isolated ostensive definitions. No doubt, that was a feature of recent reductive theories of language and its relation to the world. But there was no need to include that feature in the hypothesis of a Private Language and, when Wittgenstein does include it, the interpretation of his criticism is complicated by a question: 'how much of his critique is directed against the general hypothesis of a Private Language, and how much of it is directed against the particular version of the hypothesis that was developed by Carnap (and by Wittgenstein himself in 1929)?' (see *Philosophical Remarks*, S 58, quoted above, p. 40).

The same uncertainty affects the second, related, objection, that it is a mistake to try to introduce a word for a specific sensation, like pain, before fixing its place in language and daily life. Of course, this mistaken procedure is foisted on us by the empiricist tradition, which has always tended to combine phenomenalism with atomism. But there was no need to include the combination in the hypothesis of a Private Language, and when Wittgenstein does include it, we have to face the same question: 'How much of his critique is directed against the general hypothesis of a Private Language, and how much of it is directed against a particular version of the hypothesis—in this case the atomistic version that was favoured by empiricism?'

There is, of course, an easy way out of this problem of interpretation. We can say that his critique is directed against both targets, and that is certainly true. But it leaves an important question unanswered: if the hypothesis of a Private Language had not been associated with atomistic doctrines inherited from empiricism, would he still have rejected it? To put the question more specifically: suppose that he had not attributed to the would-be private linguist a reliance on isolated ostensive definitions or a policy of starting from simple sensory properties; would he still have rejected the hypothesis of a Private Language?

The answer to this question is undoubtedly 'Yes, he would still have rejected the hypothesis for the reason that he gives in *PI* I, S 258'. This is not to say that he had no other reasons for rejecting it or that they did not include some of the faults of contemporary empiricism. But the two faults that he did include in the target of his criticism—reliance on isolated ostensive definitions and failure to prepare a place in the language for the defined word to occupy—are not essential parts of the hypothesis of a Private Language. We can allow the would-be private linguist to reinforce his ostensive definitions by adding the subsequent applications of the defined words to sensations, and we can allow him to ensure that the order in which the different parts of his language develop is an order that would, in fact, be a possible historical order. What we cannot allow is any dilution of the would-be private linguist's central point, that his sensation-language could be established without any help from the physical world. That is the claim that Wittgenstein attacks in *PI* I, S 258, because it obliterates the distinction between being under the impression that one is reporting a sense-impression correctly and actually reporting it correctly.

This distinction has already been illustrated by an example of exteroceptive perception. You learn to recognize the colour blue by looking at blue physical objects in normal circumstances, and, if you are not colour-blind, you get a distinctive visual impression of their colour. Thereafter, when you report another visual impression of blue, the presumption is that it is caused by another blue physical object (or just by the blue sky). If I doubt this causation in spite of the fact that the circumstances of perception are normal, I can undergo a test for colour-blindness. If I fail the test, because, for example, I am blue–green colour-blind, that will show that, in my case, there is no regular connection between blue stimuli and any distinctive visual impression, and so I shall have no criterion for the application of the description 'of blue' to any of my visual impressions. If, on the other hand, I pass the test for normal colour-vision in this part of the spectrum, my spontaneous reaction to this visual impression—'it is a visual impression of blue'—will provide a sufficient reason for holding that it really is an impression of blue (and, given normal circumstances of perception, that it was caused by a blue physical object).

This account of the language of sense-impressions can be summarized in a single sentence: reports of sense-impressions are expressed in a language that is essentially dependent on reports of their causes in the physical world, including the bodies of the speakers. This fits the case of exteroceptive perception in the way that has just been described.[18]

This account is a detailed development of Wittgenstein's general characterization of the relation between language and the world:

Time and again the attempt is made to use language to limit the world and set it in relief—but it can't be done. The self-evidence of the world expresses itself in the very fact that language can and does only refer to it.

For since language only derives the way in which it means from its meaning, from the world, no language is conceivable which does not represent the world. (*PR*, S 47; quoted at greater length above, pp. 41–42)

The would-be speaker of a Private Language repudiates this source of meaning and claims a purely mental source in its place. Of course, he cannot reject the apparent facts, that we do apply words to an

---

[18] Proprioceptive cases and the special case of pain will be examined later (see below, p. 55).

independent world, and that it is only by imposing regularity on our own use of words that we discover regularities in that world. But what he can do—or what, at least, appears to be possible for him to do—is to substitute a purely mental version of those facts. So, instead of objects located in space, the phenomenalist offers the observer 'permanent possibilities of sensation' (cf. J. S. Mill, *Examination of Sir William Hamilton's Philosophy*, ch. 11) and a purely sensory itinerary which will take him to the point where the possibilities will be realized. The Kantian and neo-Kantian response to this is that it steals the advantages of an independent system of objects located in space without establishing any right to them (see G. Evans, *Things without the Mind, a Comment on Ch. 2 of Strawson's Individuals* in Evans, *Collected Papers* (Oxford, 1985) ).

Wittgenstein's response to the phenomenalization of the physical world is similar, but its point of impact is different. He shares the Kantian conviction that substituting sensations for physical objects (including our own bodies) will not give us the world as we live our lives in it. But his remedy is different. Kantian philosophy accepts the Cartesian restriction of sense-perception to objects within the mind of the percipient, and then tries to deal with the consequent impoverishment of knowledge by adding the contributions made by his mind—space, time, and the categories. This is like the advice of a doctor who says 'Your illness is incurable, but I can make it tolerable for you to live with it.' Wittgenstein's response is more radical: he tells the Cartesian patient that he can actually cure his illness, because his basic idea, that his sensations are independent objects of perception, is mistaken.

The mistake is his assumption, that the meaning of reports of exteroceptive impressions can be preserved without any reference to the objects that cause them. This assumption is a natural consequence of the Cartesian treatment of impressions. Hume, for example, observed that 'almost all mankind, and even philosophers themselves for the greatest part of their lives, take their perceptions [i.e., impressions] to be their only objects' (*Treatise* Bk I, Pt II, S 4). If this were true, the meanings of our reports of impressions would be preserved independently of any connections with physical objects, such as the connections that we use in tests for colour-blindness. But it is not true. The function of sense-impressions is to give us information about the physical world in which we have to live our lives, and so the meanings of our reports of our sense-impressions are preserved by their success in performing this role. This is conspicuously true of sensations of pain, cold, and hunger.

It is extraordinarily difficult to extract a single argument from Wittgenstein's critique of Private Language, but there does seem to be a single idea that drives it. When the incidental features contributed by Russellian empiricism and by Wittgenstein's own early theory of meaning have been removed, what lay beneath them can be seen distinctly. It is the idea that our basic needs compel us to use our linguistic techniques to measure the world, and so their constancy must be preserved. This constancy is constancy of meaning (give or take some latitude (see above, Ch. 2, p. 25 ff)). But our linguistic techniques differ from other measuring instruments in an important way. The constancy of ordinary measuring instruments can often be based on an independent test (for example, on the standard metre bar or, in the case of tempo, on a metronome), but constancy of meaning can be tested only by relying on it and seeing if it works. In the special case of sense-impressions 'working' means yielding reports that are connected in a regular way with specific physical situations. If this is circular, it is, at least, the circle of our lives.

The phenomenalist's response to the 'Private Language Argument' is to argue that it fails to make its point. No doubt, it seems to be successful in its first stage, because it is plausible to argue that there must be an independent criterion[19] of the truth of a report of a visual impression. This is plausible because our sensory apparatus has to deliver reliable information about the world in which we live, and so, *to that extent*, it is like a battery of physical measuring instruments that need to be tested on our environment and calibrated. However, our senses are also, in another way, very unlike physical measuring instruments: they cannot be removed by surgery and tested on a work-bench. They can only be tested in working order in their place between the physical world and our construal and use of the physical world. 'The world and life are one.'[20] So the test of a person's colour-vision simply reverses his use of his colour-vision: he uses it to discover the colour of a physical object, but the tester uses a physical object with an independently known colour in order to discover the discriminatory power of his colour-vision.

---

[19] i.e., there must be an independent criterion to be used when someone is learning the language. When he has learned it, he will not have to check his technique every time that he reports a visual impression of blue. On the contrary, he will rely on his technique and claim that the physical cause of his visual impression really is blue. If he always checked his basic technique in the way in which we check for colour-blindness, it would not serve its purpose. The normal flow of inference is from impression to cause, in spite of the fact that the report of the visual impression is not incorrigible and must sometimes be checked against the cause that produces it.

[20] *TLP*, 5.621.

It is the second stage of the 'Private Language Argument' that the phenomenalist rejects. The second stage is the claim that this account of the relation between the language of sensations and the language of physical objects cannot be reduced to a purely phenomenal version in which physical objects figure only as 'permanent possibilities of sensation' (J. S. Mill's formulation of phenomenalism in *Examination of Sir William Hamilton's Philosophy* (London, 1865, ch. 11). The phenomenalist simply rejects this criticism and argues that Wittgenstein's account of the relations between language, sensations, and the physical world really can be reformulated without loss in purely sensory terms. So when Wittgenstain requires a physical check for a report of a sensation, the phenomenalist responds by offering, instead, a sensory check, consisting of the sensations to which, in his theory, the physical check has been reduced (see A. J. Ayer, *Wittgenstein*, (Random House, New York), pp. 75 ff.).

The main objection to this response is the contention that a purely sensory sequence, terminating with the actualization of possible sensations, is an inadequate substitute for a journey in space terminating with an encounter with the object that caused the sensations. A flat pattern is no substitute for a picture with depth, especially when the picture has to include the body of its perceiving subject. There are two ways of developing this objection. One way is to describe the complexities of the system of physical objects, including our own bodies, in space (see G. Evans 'Things Without the Mind' (in *Collected Papers*, OUP 1985)). The other way is to dwell on the inadequacies of a purely sensory analysis of that system. The 'Private Language Argument' takes the second line of criticism.

The target of this criticism is the phenomenalist's facile assumption that meaning can be preserved within his minimalist picture. But how will it be preserved? He simply assumes that the checks that are available in the physical world can be transferred without any essential change to the phenomenal world. The only change would be that, instead of checking a report of a sensation against its physical cause, he will now have to check it against the sequence of sensations to which the physical cause will have been reduced. But, according to him, that is not an essential change.

Wittgenstein's objection to this is that the phenomenalist's substitution of sensations for physical objects *is* an essential change. It is essential because the preservation of meaning and the sharing of meaning stand or fall together. Both are made possible by a single, crucial condition—that meaning is preserved by objects accessible to anyone in the relevant community of language-speakers. Sensations do not satisfy this condition, but it is satisfied by the contents of the physical world. If this condition is mandatory for communication between different speakers of the same language, it follows immediately that a private language is an impossibility. For the lack of any set of objects that might have made communication possible will automatically remove the possibility that a solitary speaker might be able to preserve the meanings of his words. It is no good appealing to definitions at this point, because they merely postpone the day of reckoning, when we shall stand at the interface between language and the world. That is the general point that he made in *Philosophical Remarks*, S 47 (see above, pp. 41–42) and it is the point that he develops in *Philosophical Investigations* I, S 258. This is an essentially simple and powerful argument. It does not rely on the dubious assumption that a language must actually be shared and could not be invented by a solitary speaker.[21] All that it requires is that the meanings of its words must be preserved by their regular application to things in the physical world which would be accessible to other people if there were any other people around. To put the point in another way, self-revelation is essentially a secondary function of language. The best indication of this order of linguistic development is the simple fact, so easily forgotten by those who follow Descartes's lead, that we have to use coloured objects to test people's colour-vision.

Although this is a powerful argument, it has been handicapped by its tendency to produce misunderstandings and invalid responses. One such response has already been mentioned. People say, 'I'm sure that I could set up a Private Language in the original position described by Carnap.' But they are merely imagining themselves with all their present sophistication and familiarity with the relations between the language of sensations and the language of physical objects, and taking all this intellectual equipment with them on a visit to Carnap's 'original position' (see above, p. 44).

This is an obviously invalid response to the 'Private Language Argument'. But even the standard phenomenalist response is really no more convincing. That response is to argue that the reduction of physical objects to sense-data still leaves the phenomenalist in a position to check his reports of his sensations against their physical context. The only difference is that the physical context will now be specified in sensory terms, and so he will be checking one sensory statement against a group

---

[21] See below, pp. 60–63.

of sensory statements, categorical and hypothetical. But this misses the point of Wittgenstein's objection. Its point is not that the would-be private linguist cannot formulate a test of his report of a sensation. He can formulate such a test, but only in words that exploit the illusion that meaning could be preserved in a language that had severed all its connections with the physical world in order to achieve privacy. But how would it be preserved? By unchecked memory?

Pain is a special case, very different from a visual impression of a colour, and more needs to be said about its peculiarities. There is a shift of emphasis between the development of the 'Private Language Argument' in the 1936 lectures and its development in *Philosophical Investigations*. In the 1936 lectures more space is allotted to exteroceptive impressions, and in the later work there is more emphasis on pain. It is worth asking why this is so.

Sceptical arguments against the veracity of sense-perception from Sextus Empiricus to Galileo had always tried to exploit the peculiarity of pain. If we do not locate pain in the painful stimulus, why should we locate colour in the object that gives us visual impressions of colour? The answer must be that the two concepts, *painful* and *blue*, have different structures. A painful sensation may have various causes, but it has a fairly uniform behavioural effect—complaint and avoidance; whereas an impression of blue has a single, specific cause and no uniform behavioural effect. This difference provides us with an explanation of the fact that we do not call the surfaces of physical objects 'painful' in the flat, unqualified way in which we would call an object 'blue'. Objects can be painful to touch, or painful to swallow, but not painful *tout court* (cf. *PI* I, S 312), but if they are blue they are simply and flatly blue (cf. *PI* I, S 276, discussed below, p. 56 ff.). This difference makes pain a good example for Wittgenstein to use in the controversy about Private Language. For the public character of reports of pain follows from the simplest way of teaching a child the meaning of the word; which is to introduce it as a substitute for the natural expression of pain.

For how can I go so far as to try to use language to get between pain and its expression? (*PI* I, S 245)

If anyone doubts the reliability of natural expressions of pain when they are used as criteria, it will be a sufficient response to point out that complete insensitivity to pain is more likely than complete stoicism (see *PI* I, 257 and 288).

However, there are three puzzling features of the 'Private Language Argument'. First, reports of sensations are supposed to be unlike reports of physical objects in the following way: the person who has the sensation and reports it does not rely on a criterion, but does have a right to report it (*PI* I, S 189). What gives him the right? Second, if someone suggests that his right is based on the fact that it is an object confronting him in his mind, Wittgenstein's response is dismissive. 'Always get rid of the private object in this way: assume that it constantly changes but you don't notice the changes because your memory constantly deceives you' (*PI* II, p. 207). This suggestion sounds like overkill, because if it really could be used to eliminate the private object, it seems that it could be used to eliminate something that actually did occur in the mind of a person who perceived a physical object. Third, Wittgenstein's verdict on the possibility of a solitary language is unclear. Did he think that the absence of other people would make it impossible for someone solitary from birth to develop a language (for his own thoughts and for recording memoranda)? Or did he think that his relations with the physical world would still provide him with a sufficient basis for developing a solitary language?

We may start by considering the first of these three problems: the question of criteria and rights. If a person's reports of his own sensations lack a criterion of truth, he must be relying on something else when he makes them. If he is relying on his right to make them, there must be something that gives him that right. The minimal condition that would suffice to establish his right is his having learned to report the sensation when, and very nearly only when, he has it. So other people teach him this lesson indirectly by using the outward criteria of stimulus and response. If the lesson takes hold and he acquires the technique of responding autonomously to his sensations by applying the appropriate words to them, he graduates. After his graduation, we might wonder whether his reports will be infallible. However, Wittgenstein never proposed at this point the general doctrine of infallibility that some of his contemporaries proposed. He merely observed that we would not know what to make of a person who said that he did not know whether a sensation that he now had was pain (*PI* I, S 288).

This minimalist account of sensation-language is frequently mistaken for crude behaviourism, and Wittgenstein often returns to the task of rebutting that interpretation. A sensation, sandwiched between stimulus and response, is not like a beetle in a collector's box (*PI* I, S 293), and an impression of a colour is not like a detachable membrane reproducing the colour of the object beneath it (*PI* I, S 276). The whole tide of thought about perception since the seventeenth century had been flowing in the wrong direction so consistently that any attempt to correct it was taken to be a denial of the obvious instead of a new way of thinking about the obscure.

However, it must be admitted that some of his remarks about sensations seem to be too paradoxical to be salvaged in this way. For example, it is not easy to understand his discussion of people who can tell by sensation that their blood-pressure is going up. What he says about this kind of case is this:

> Let us now imagine a use for the entry of the sign 'S' in my diary. I discover that, whenever I have a particular sensation, a manometer shows that my blood-pressure rises. So I shall be able to say that my blood-pressure is rising without using any apparatus. This is a useful result.   (*PI*, S 270)

So far, so good. This is now a case of a report of a sensation achieving a connection with the physical world in a way that not only stabilizes it but also provides useful information about my body. But he continues:

> And now it seems quite indifferent whether I have recognized the sensation *right* or not. Let us suppose I regularly identify it wrong; it does not matter in the least. And that alone shows that the hypothesis that I make a mistake is mere show. (We, as it were, turned a knob which looked as if it could be used to turn on some part of the machine, but it was a mere ornament, not connected with the mechanism at all.)   (Ibid.)

This is a paradoxical thing to say, given that it is through my sensation that I recognize that my blood-pressure is rising. His point must be, that then, is the way to put it, and that it is a mistake to say that I recognize the property of the sensation. For that suggests that my sensation is an object with a property recognizable independently of this particular connection with the physical world. For example, it might have been like the feeling of tension behind the forehead (not quite a headache) that some people get when a thunderstorm is approaching. But his point is that it is not like that. For when I discover through sensation that my blood-pressure is rising, my sensation does not already have an independently recognizable phenomenal property. Its only property is the one whose discovery is described in this text, namely, the property of indicating a rise in my blood-pressure. So I begin by saying 'I have a strange feeling' and then, when I discover the connection with rising blood-pressure, I use it to describe what I feel. It is not at all surprising that I cannot give a phenomenal description of the feeling that will serve as its basic identification.

This topic, the emergence of descriptions of sensations, is shrouded in fog. We feel that sensations must have phenomenal properties, through which they are first identified and that any informative properties that they may acquire will be superimposed on them later. This leads us to exaggerate the definiteness and detail of the original phenomenal identification, and to treat the informative properties of a sensation as inessential after-thoughts. Wittgenstein's critique of the 'Private Object' is a sustained attack on this prejudice. Sensations and impressions are often first identified by their informative properties and not by their phenomenal properties. A visual impression is not *blue* but *of blue*. We see the blue object through it and this tempts us to say that it is itself blue, but only in the way in which a pane of glass through which we see the blue sky is blue (cf. Wittgenstein's analogy—a detachable membrane, *PI* I, S 276).

We do not have to choose between restricting the properties of sensations to one of the two categories, phenomenal or informative. Wittgenstein treats their informative properties as basic in *PI*, S 258. That does not mean that they lack phenomenal properties, but it does reduce the pressure of the prejudice that they all ought to be immediately identifiable through their phenomenal properties. It also neutralizes another prejudice: we do not have to suppose that informativeness depends on copying (the relation that captivated European philosophers for so many centuries), and we are set free to explore the way in which it depends on regular connections between type of sensation and type of stimulus. That is the main point of Wittgenstein's critique of the 'Private Object'.

A child might imagine that light travels down the wire that connects the switch with an electric lamp. Anaxagoras believed that a dog is composed of minute dog-shaped atoms (a primitive anticipation of modern genetic theory). This pattern of explanation is especially persuasive in the philosophy of perception and the reason why it is so persuasive is clear: if I can be mistaken about the physical object that I think I see, I shall be on similar, but much safer, ground if I confine myself to making a claim about my visual impression of it. So the complete chain of perception connecting an observer to a physical object is taken to contain a shorter segment which reproduces its structure on a smaller scale. When Wittgenstein rejects this assumption it is not at all surprising that he is often taken to be denying something obvious. But what he is denying is not even true.

The right substitute for copying is regular connection, which is sufficient in itself and is allowed to be sufficient in the case of many scientific measuring instruments. So why should we expect anything better of our own perceptual apparatus? That neutralizes the paradoxical flavour of Wittgenstein's summing up of the case of the person who discovers that his sensation S, hitherto a stray sensation, is, in fact, regularly connected with a rise in his blood-pressure. The problematical part of his diagnosis is his claim that

... now it seems quite indifferent whether I have recognized the sensation *right* or not. Let us suppose I regularly identify it wrong, it does not matter in the least. And that alone shows that the hypothesis that I make a mistake is mere show. (We, as it were, turned a knob which looked as if it could be used to turn on some part of the machine; but it was a mere ornament, not connected with the machine at all.) ... (*PI* I, S 270; quoted at greater length, above, p. 57)

This should be compared with a similar remark that he makes in his discussion of seeing aspects:

Always get rid of the idea of a private object in this way: assume that it constantly changes, but that you do not notice the changes because your memory constantly deceives you. (*PI* II, xi. p. 207)

In this case the 'Private Object' is the visual impression that is supposed to explain our seeing the puzzle-picture as a rabbit rather than a duck.

This sounds like overkill, because it seems that it could be used to eliminate something that really did occur in the field of consciousness of a person perceiving a physical object. All that you have to do is to imagine that, whatever that thing is, it acquires a misleading property which you fail to notice and so are not misled. But Wittgenstein's argument need not be given such a devastating interpretation. Instead of *proving* that a proposed link in the chain of perception would be irrelevant, it might merely *suggest* that conclusion by presenting a situation in which the thing that really mattered, regular connection, was preserved and the thing that did not matter, facsimile representation, was jettisoned. The question that is implicit in this treatment of the chain of perception is this: 'can you honestly say that this suggestion leaves out anything that is essential to perception?' Perception measures the world, but the instrument that it uses does not have to produce replicas of what it is used to measure. To put the point in another way, if we insist on foreshortening the view into the world that is yielded by perception, we ought not to expect that it will terminate on objects of the same kind, just as we ought not to expect to find light in an electric wire when we cut it short. (But, of course, this comparison uses an analogue in which the flow of causation is reversed.)

We may still feel puzzled by the fact that Wittgenstein ends his discussion of the connection between the sensation S and a rise in my blood-pressure by saying, 'so I shall be able to say that my blood-pressure is rising without using my apparatus. This is a useful result' (*PI* I, S 270, quoted above, p. 57). This conclusion is surprising because we expect him to conclude that we can now establish 'S' as a word with a meaning by finding a regular connection between it and something in the physical world. For that was what was lacking before and needed in order to give 'S' a meaning. But he focuses instead on a special consequence of the achievement of meaning in this particular case: I shall be able to tell immediately when my blood-pressure is rising. Perhaps this is ironical: we naturally think of the useful consequence in this special case and overlook the underlying general consequence—meaning has been achieved. His discussion would have been easier to understand if he had pointed out that the two consequences depend on two different uses of the same sensation. Meaning is achieved when the sensation is correlated with a rise in blood-pressure: that is an example of the kind of stabilizing connection that is required in *PI* I, S 258. Truth is achieved when I use this connection in a particular case to infer the rise in blood-pressure from the sensation.

The third and last problem posed by the interpretation of the 'Private Language Argument' was a problem about the two conditions that make it possible to set up a language—connection with the physical world and communication with other people. Did Wittgenstein think that language would be impossible only if it lacked *both* the advantages of an ordinary language—i.e., both the possibility of communicating with other people and the possibility of discovering regularities in the world around us? Or would it be disqualified as a language if it just happened never to be shared with anyone else because there were never any other people around? We may call this a 'solitary language' and its speaker 'Super-Crusoe'. (Crusoe himself had not been solitary from birth, but only between being shipwrecked and meeting Man Friday.)[22]

So we may ask whether Wittgenstein believed that Super-Crusoe could have developed a language for his own use in making physical records and in developing his thoughts about his environment. Before

[22] See C. Verheggen, 'Wittgenstein and "Solitary" Languages', *Philosophical Investigations*, 18/4 (October, 1995), 329–47.

we seek Wittgenstein's answer to that question, we need to be clear about its meaning. It does not mean, 'could he have developed a language that nobody could decipher?' If anthropologists discovered him after years of his life as a solitary castaway, and if they succeeded in deciphering his language, that would not show that it had not been a solitary language before they found him. It would only show that it was not a Private, or necessarily unteachable, Language. Whatever the disadvantages of the solitude in which he had been living previously, they would not be removed retrospectively by the later sharing of his language with his discoverers.[23]

The two deprivations—one of human company alone, and the other of the physical world including human company—needed to be assessed by Wittgenstein before he gave his verdict on a Private Language. But what exactly was his assessment? Were both the supports necessary? If so, which of the two supports was more important and its loss, therefore, more disabling?

The baffling feature of his investigation is that he treats these questions as marginal. They are questions that other philosophers ask because they want to know the necessary conditions of speaking a language, but his interest may be different. He appears not to be seeking a theory about the essence of language but to be more concerned with describing the multifariousness of our linguistic practices than with the possibility of putting them in a rigid frame. Nevertheless, his descriptive work inevitably raises the questions that he treats as marginal, and if we want to know his attitude to them, we shall have to cast our net more widely. If we want to know whether he believed a solitary language to be an impossibility, we need to look again at his account of following a linguistic rule. Did he think that it required a regularity preserved by the speech of more than one person? There is no clear answer to that question in *Philosophical Investigations*. Yet it must be an important question, because, if the distinction really would vanish in a solitary language, that would show that language would be impossible without intercourse between people.

But on that point he hedges his claim:

If language is to be a means of communication, there must be agreement not only in definitions, but also (queer as it may sound), in judgements. (*PI*, I S 242)

---

[23] A point made by several commentators. See my *The False Prison*, ii. 374.

There is a parallel, but more explanatory, passage in *Remarks on the Foundations of Mathematics*:

> We say that, in order to communicate, people must agree with one another about the meanings of words. But the criterion for this agreement is not just agreement with reference to definitions, e.g. ostensive definitions—but *also* agreement in judgements. It is essential for communication that we agree in a large number of judgements.   (*RFM* VI, S 39)

But what if there is nobody else with whom to communicate? Would Super-Crusoe's solitary vocalizations necessarily fail to count as a language? Wittgenstein side-steps this question and asks, instead, the related question, whether it would be possible that there should have been only one occasion on which someone obeyed a rule (sc. a linguistic rule). He gives this question an unqualified negative answer, and he takes the same line about mathematical calculation:

> But what about the consensus? Doesn't it mean that *one* human being by himself could not calculate? Well, *one* human being could, at any rate, not calculate just *once* in his life.   (*RFM* III, S 67)

These are evasions. What they parry is the demand for crisp, sharp-edged definitions of calculating or speaking a language. The reason for not meeting the demand is that these concepts do not have structures that can be cut out and pinned down in the classical way. Even when there is a clearly discernible centre, there will often be lines radiating out from it in different directions with no clear termini. Naturally, the central point of the concept of language is that it is a medium for communication between people, but thinking often uses language and Plato described it as the soul's dialogue with itself. Of course, he meant the thinking of people who already used their language to communicate with one another, and Super-Crusoe's predicament would be more extreme. Did Wittgenstein maintain that, therefore, he could not have a language? Perhaps there is no need to draw a rigid line around the circumference and it may be sufficient if we mark the zones in which the concept shades off into inapplicability. However, the need for standardization and the drilling of our children in conformity lie near the centre of the concept. So perhaps Wittgenstein's enquiry could be put like this: 'How far from the centre can a philosophical thesis about the necessary conditions of language move without becoming unacceptable?', and it might become unacceptable before it became outright nonsense. So in *Philosophical Investigations* he says that his method is to describe a movement of thought rather than to identify a definite point at which sense is lost.

My aim is to teach you to pass from a piece of disguised nonsense to something that is patent nonsense. (*PI*, S 464)

The only firm conclusion that can be drawn from his discussion of the use of language as a means of communication is that it must be sharable, even if it is not actually shared.

When *Philosophical Investigations* was published in 1953, most philosophers found its method baffling. Instead of hammering a problem into a readily decidable shape and then forcing a solution to it, Wittgenstein always moved back to an earlier stage in the enquiry, the stage at which relevant material is collected. What he collected were ordinary patterns of speech and thought, and his idea was that the shape of a complex concept was something that could only be traced delicately and incompletely in that material. Abstraction was falsification and the search for simple solutions, which had been so successful in science, was a failure in philosophy. It is not surprising that, when *Philosophical Investigations* first appeared, its readers seized on 'The Private Language Argument' (itself a simplifying misnomer) and read it as an attempt to substitute a new theory for earlier rivals. They wanted a definite theory, but what he offered was something more impressionistic.

If we must identify a central point in his treatment of perception and language, an equally good candidate would be the combination of the two ideas whose problematic connection I have now postponed for too long. One was the idea that linguistic techniques are the repositories of meaning, and the other was the idea that the two stages that are distinct when we are describing physical objects, knowing how to apply a word and knowing the criterion of its correct application are often syncopated when we are reporting our own sensations.[24] Both these ideas are examples of theoretical compression. It is so natural for philosophers to model what goes on in our minds on what goes on in the physical world in our immediate vicinity, and both Wittgenstein's leading ideas make the same kind of contribution to a more parsimonious and realistic description of the mental scene. The usual distinction between measurer and measuring instrument collapses under the pressure of his treatment

---

[24] See above, Ch. 1, pp. 2–3, for Wittgenstein's account of our bafflement when we know how to apply a word to a sensation but cannot give any criterion of its correct application. We begin to stammer.

of linguistic regularity, and the usual distinction between knowing how to apply a word and knowing the criterion of its correct application collapses under the pressure of his criticism of the assimilation of sensations to objects.

Of course, these two examples of theoretical compression are very different in kind. One eliminates the suggestion that meaning resides in a thing that is either in the speaker's mind or in the world outside it; while the other eliminates the suggestion that the speaker uses a separable objective mark to guide his application of a word to sensations. But both of them destroy the illusion that there is a way of escaping our alarming responsibility for unformulatable accuracy. We have to accept the human predicament, which does, after all, allow us a certain freedom of choice.

# 4

# Logical Necessity

What is the force of logical necessity? Why do we infer $q$ from $p$ and *if p, then q* so slavishly? And why are we so confident that *if* $\sim q$, *then* $\sim p$ must also be true? Or that the same coloured surface cannot be both entirely red and entirely green? These are questions about the source of the compulsion that we feel and about what it is like to feel it, and so right from the start the inquiry is balanced between reality and our reactions to reality. Our inferences and the tracks that they follow raise questions very like the question discussed in Chapter 2: 'What is the explanation of the extension of a general word?' However, this time these questions are going to be more difficult to answer.

There are several reasons for their greater difficulty. One reason—perhaps the most important one—is that the logical necessities that we recognize seem to be the indispensable conditions of all thought, like the air that we breathe, and we find it hard to imagine continuing to think without them. This produces a big difference between these questions about the foundations of logic and the question discussed in Chapter 2. For the application of any general word might well have been different from what it now is, and it is often easy to imagine circumstances in which it really would have been different. In fact, there are many cases where we can actually see a word developing a new extension to its old meaning and we can often understand why it does so. But logic seems to be made of harder stuff, and that is the main reason why Wittgenstein's anthropocentric treatment of it is more difficult to accept, and even to understand, than his anthropocentric treatment of the regular application of general words.

There are also two further reasons for the greater difficulty of his account of logical necessity. One is that its Conventionalism, with its strong hint of artificiality, steals the limelight, while its Voluntarism, which has no such implication, stands behind it in the shadows and fails to cancel the implication of capriciousness.[1] The other, more general, reason is that both his Conventionalism and his Voluntarism seem to be inconsistent with his rejection of all theorizing in philosophy (see *PI* I, S 109, quoted above, p. ix and p. 17). These two stumbling-blocks are connected in a way that will be explained briefly now, and their importance will emerge later in the detailed exposition of his account of logical necessity.

His account is usually presented as a Conventionalist alternative to Realism. This is correct about what it denies but incomplete about what it asserts. He denies that valid logical inferences track logical necessities that already exist independently of anything that we may do. But this denial needs to be supplemented with an account of the rationality of the way in which we come to accept the validity of patterns of logical inference, especially when the patterns of inference are new. If the denial is left without that supplement, our acceptance of new patterns will seem to be merely capricious. He certainly thought that our acceptance of innovations is arbitrary rather than forced on us by a real necessity existing independently of anything that we might do. But he did not think that it is capricious. Of course, the new pattern will be an innovation, but he thought that it would be an innovation that develops naturally out of an old way of thinking. This is rational Voluntarism rather than capricious Conventionalism, and it provides him with a new way of interpreting proof in logic.[2]

If Wittgenstein's Voluntarism really were entirely capricious, the adoption of a new rule of logical inference would be unintelligible. Humpty-Dumpty said: 'It's my word and I can do what I like with it', and he could also have said, 'these are my sentences and I can connect them in any way I like'. '*Hoc volo, sic jubeo, sit pro ratione voluntas*'. But that, of course, really would be absurd. Pure spontaneity is not an acceptable alternative to Realism in this area. If we put a new rule of inference in the archive for future use, we must have a reason for putting it there (see *RFM* III, 29–31).

But this raises a difficult problem. It is clear that Wittgenstein wished to steer a course somewhere between the idea that we discover logical

---

[1] Descartes maintained that the acceptance of any truth, contingent or necessary, was an act of will. That did not imply that it was capricious, but it was not easy to find a convincing alternative explanation of necessary truths.

[2] See below, p. 76 ff.

necessities and the idea that we create them, but much closer to the idea that we create them. For Realism can only say that our logically valid inferences track real necessities and that does not succeed in explaining our techniques of logical inference any more than the Realist's appeal to universals succeeded in explaining our techniques of applying general words to things. On the other hand, in both areas Conventionalism without any mention of reasons would obviously concede too much to spontaneity, because in both areas it would leave the field wide open to caprice. However, the reason adduced by the Realist to explain our applications of general words—they track universals—are merely a projection of the practices that they are supposed to explain. For the universals that were conscripted to support our applications of general words would not be independently identifiable. Similarly, there would be no independent way of identifying the real necessities that our preferred patterns of logical inference might be supposed to track. In both cases a different kind of explanation is needed.

However, the general rejection of empty theories of this kind still leaves open the possibility that philosophy might be able to appeal to theories of another, more substantial, kind. That is a possibility that Wittgenstein himself was going to exploit. For, as will emerge later, he gave an apparently historical account of our adoption of new rules of inference. But how are we meant to understand his account? Is it meant as a factual contribution to historical anthropology? Or is it a deconstruction of our present situation which explains it by showing how it must have developed. But what is the justification of the word 'must'? This is an issue that has haunted philosophy since the Renaissance. If an account of the origin of a problematic phenomenon is not literally true, what are the criteria of its acceptability? Are there explanations with one foot in the factual world and the other in a speculative reconstruction of indispensable origins?

In any case, Wittgenstein's outright rejection of all theorizing in philosophy (*PI* I, S 109, quoted and discussed above, pp. ix and 17) certainly needs to be limited in some way. His opposition to theories that offer empty explanations of familiar phenomena is understandable, and such explanations are only too common in philosophy. But all theories? Must philosophy always be purely descriptive? That is a much more audacious claim. However, the main obstacle to understanding his treatment of logical necessity is its implication that there is anything optional about it. There are obvious options about the applications of general words, but we simply feel forced to accept a valid logical inference. How, then, can the assimilation of two such different cases possibly loosen the grip of the Realist's interpretation of logic?

It is a good policy to start the detailed investigation of his treatment of logical necessity by fixing its general character, which is fully formed in his later writings, but already nascent in the *Tractatus* and in *Notebooks 1914–1916*. In all his discussions, early and late, he tried to build up logic from its foundations in the everyday thinking of ordinary people instead of developing it from the top downwards by hanging all its theorems on a minimal set of axioms and rules of inference. John Locke said that it did not take Aristotle to make men rational (*Essay Concerning Human Understanding*, Bk IV, ch. 17), and Wittgenstein could have said the same of Frege and Russell.

In the *Tractatus* he argued that all necessary truths are tautologies, and that answers the question about their nature in a way that by-passes the enterprise of proving them in a calculus. So in his early work he gave proof in logic a minor role and treated it not as an essential support of necessary truths but only as a way of identifying tautologies in difficult cases:

Proof in logic is merely a mechanical expedient to facilitate the recognition of tautologies in complicated cases.   (*TLP*, 6. 1262)

His idea, that necessary truths are essentially tautological, seems to have been inspired by Schopenhauer's treatment of geometry. For Schopenhauer had belittled the need for Euclid's proofs and relied on spatial intuition to establish each theorem by separate inspection. That is very close to Wittgenstein's idea, that we can see all the implications of a proposition in the proposition itself, and if what we see is that it is a tautology—i.e., that it is true whatever the truth-values of its components—we see that it is necessarily true:

A proposition constructs a world with the help of a logical scaffolding, so that one can actually see from the proposition how everything stands logically *if* it is true   (*TLP*, 4.023)

When tautology is used as a criterion of necessary truth, it is a great leveller. For there is no further characteristic that entitles some necessary truths to be treated as axioms, while others have to be deduced from them.

All the propositions of logic are of equal status: it is not the case that some of them are essentially primitive propositions, and others are essentially derived propositions.

Every tautology itself shows that it is a tautology. (*TLP*, 6. 127)

So every logically necessary proposition is independently recognizable as such.

It is the peculiar mark of logical propositions that one can recognize that they are true from the symbol alone, and this fact contains in itself the whole philosophy of logic.... (*TLP*, 6. 113)

It is probable that this treatment of logical necessity was inspired by Schopenhauer's discussion of geometrical necessity in *The World as Will and Idea*. For Schopenhauer criticized Euclid's axiomatization of geometry in the same way that Wittgenstein criticizes the axiomatization of logic:

In order to improve the method of mathematics, it is especially necessary to overcome the prejudice that demonstrated truth has any superiority over what is known through perception. (Schopenhauer, *The World as Will and Idea*, tr. R. B. Haldane and J. Kemp (Routledge & Kegan Paul, 1883) i. 96)

A little later he explains:

Whoever denies the necessity exhibited for intuition or perception of the space-relations expressed in any proposition, may just as well deny the axioms or that the conclusion follows from the premisses ... For anyone to wish to derive the necessity of space-relations, known in intuition or perception, from the principle of contradiction by means of a logical demonstration, is just the same as for the feudal superior of an estate to wish to hold it as the vassal of another. Yet this is what Euclid has done. His axioms only he is compelled to leave resting on immediate evidence; ... (Ibid., 97)

Schopenhauer is, of course, criticizing reliance on proofs in a geometrical calculus and he is not questioning the use of geometrical theorems as rules of inference to establish contingent conclusions from contingent premisses in daily life. Similarly, Wittgenstein is criticizing reliance on proofs *in* logic and he is not questioning the use of logical theorems as rules of inference to establish contingent conclusions from contingent premisses in daily life. In his later work he changed his mind and conceded greater importance to proof in logic, but he always retained the idea that they must be completely perspicuous (see *RFM* III, 1 and 39). The effect of his early reading of Schopenhauer runs very deep in his philosophy.

The main importance of Wittgenstein's idea, that the truths of logic are tautologies, is sufficiently obvious. It provided an answer to the question, how the axioms and rules of inference used in a calculus could be justified—a convincing answer at least for the propositional calculus. But, at the same time, it provided an independent test for the necessary truth of the theorems and that made the calculus redundant. So Wittgenstein, like Schopenhauer and unlike Euclid, treated the construction of calculi as an optional pastime.

This is connected with an important feature of Wittgenstein's early treatment of logic that has already been mentioned (see above, p. 68). It is a very clear manifestation of the policy of building up logic from its foundations in the everyday thinking of ordinary people. For it ties its development to the intentions of a speaker who makes an ordinary contingent statement. What such a person says will be intended to be compatible with some glosses but incompatible with others, and, according to the theory of meaning of the *Tractatus*, these connections will be made manifest in the analysis of the sentence that he utters. The ingenuity required in order to construct a calculus that would systematize the rules of inference that he uses simply is not needed. As he says in an early entry in the *Notebooks*, 'Logic must take care of itself' (*NB*, 22-viii-14).

Many commentators on the development of Wittgenstein's philosophy assume that the project of building up logic from its foundations in the everyday thinking of ordinary people belongs exclusively to his later philosophy. But the fact is that it started with his early idea that all logically necessary propositions are tautologies. The logical implications of a proposition are actually contained in the proposition itself as it stands on the page and they will be displayed in its analysis:

A proposition must restrict reality to two alternatives: yes or no.

In order to do that, it must describe reality completely.

A proposition is a description of a state of affairs.

Just as a description of an object describes it by giving its external properties, so a proposition describes reality by its internal properties.

A proposition constructs a world with the help of a logical scaffolding, so that one can actually see from the proposition how everything stands logically *if* it is true. One can *draw inferences* from a false proposition.   (*TLP*, 4.023)

Tautologies are a limiting case: we can see that they come out true for all assignments of truth-value to their component propositions.

Later, when he conceded to proof in logic some of its traditional importance, Schopenhauer's influence still made itself felt. For he required proofs in logic to be perspicuous, like the diagrams that accompany proofs in geometry (see above, pp. 68–69). However, this aspect of his treatment of logic was over-determined, because it was as much the effect of his own natural tendency to use diagrams and mechanical analogies to express his ideas. Spatiality was never far below the surface of his thinking.

The controversy between Realists and Conventionalists about the necessity of the truths of logic never looked likely to end in a straight-forward victory for either side. It is not difficult to see that this is because in this case we can have no conception of reality in its raw, unconceptualized state. Of course, we can talk about it and pretend that we know what our words mean, but if we are challenged to say what we mean, we can only respond with advice to subtract: take your present world-view and subtract your own intellectual contribution to it. If we are asked what would be left, we can only repeat the advice and we cannot specify what the remainder would be like.

This is a clear demonstration of the special character of the limit of language and thought: you cannot stand just inside it and use language to describe what lies outside it. Epicurus argued that the universe must be infinite because, if it had a limit, you could always walk up to it and throw a spear beyond it. But if anyone used a similar argument to prove that language has no limits, the most plausible response would be that it has limits but what lies on the other side of them would simply be nonsense (*TLP*, Preface, 3).[3]

Nevertheless, we could always introduce a linguistic innovation that would push the limits further out beyond their present position. We could also use language as it stood before the innovation to present reasons for adopting the innovation. But what we could never do would be to take the raw, unconceptualized material which our language has assimilated, and describe it as it was before it was assimilated.[4]

---

[3] The spatial analogy inherent in the concept of a limit is radically misleading. The limit of language is unique because on the far side of it there is nothing (see below p. 84). That sounds as if it means that on the far side of it there are only the kind of absences that produce false propositions. But what it means is more radical than that: it means that there are not even any unrealized possibilities on the far side of the limit of language. So words fail us when we try to describe this rarefied zone and its minimalized contents. It is more extreme than a void and more like a vacuum, a logical vacuum devoid not only of facts but also of possibilities and so impervious to Epicurus' spear.

This is the point where the realism of the *Tractatus* seems to peter out. But really it is only the spatial image that fails us. We cannot treat its shortfall as a point in favour of Idealism. For when someone seeks a reason for adding a new possibility to the possibilities that he already recognizes, the reason must be based on something outside his mind.

[4] When Socrates is describing his new method of division in the *Phaedrus* he makes a similar observation: division must come to an end somewhere and at that point we must let things go on their unlimited way (*Phaedrus*, 265 ff.).

This is a limitation of a unique kind. We know that our applications of general words to things and our acknowledgements of logical necessities must be the joint products of reality and our reactions to reality, but we have no general way of separating the contributions made by the two donors. This produces a unique situation in which the competition for recognition is intense, but the material required to adjudicate it is necessarily unavailable. In one of Wittgenstein's two cases this situation is not so very frustrating: we can readily appreciate the emptiness of the Realist's rigid explanation of our applications of general words, and we can accept Wittgenstein's substitution of volatile techniques, which developed in ways that are open to scientific explanation. But in his other case, logical necessity, it is much more difficult to accept his alternative to Realism. It sounds too subjective, too capricious.

However, though it is easy to express dissatisfaction with the apparent subjectivity of his later treatment of logical necessity, it is not so easy to understand it. Perhaps the best policy would be to start with the account that he gives in the *Tractatus* and to try to identify the reasons for his later changes of mind. This might make the transition from his earlier to his later treatment of logic more intelligible.

In the *Tractatus* he presented the problem posed by the existence of logical necessities in a very stark way:

> 5.552 The 'experience' that we need in order to understand logic is not that something or other is the state of things, but that something *is*: that, however, is *not* an experience.
>
> Logic is *prior* to every experience—that something *is so*.
>
> It is prior to the question 'How?', not prior to the question 'What?'
>
> 5.5521 And if this were not so, how could we apply logic? We might put it in this way: if there would be a logic even if there were no world, how then could there be a logic given that there is a world?   (*TLP*, 5.552–5–5.5521)

If logic was not constructed to fit the actual world, how can it avoid a conflict with it?

His solution to this problem was that logically necessary propositions are tautologies which say nothing and so are compatible with anything that the world can offer us as reality. This is just as well because 'Logic must take care of itself' (*NB*, 22-viii-14), and, *pace* Russell, it can never presuppose the existence of facts of any specific structure (see *TLP*, 5.55–5.5571). If it did not limit its commitments in this way, it would be weakened by including hostages to contingency and so could not justify its claim to necessity.

This sounds like a total rejection of Realism in this area, but, in fact, his position was less extreme. For in the *Tractatus* he went on to develop a kind of Vestigial Realism about the foundations of the tautologies of logic.

> The propositions of logic describe the scaffolding of the world, or rather they represent it. They have no 'subject-matter'. They presuppose that names have meaning and elementary propositions sense; and that is their connection with the world. It is clear that something about the world must be indicated by the fact that certain combinations of symbols—whose essence involves the possession of a determinate character—are tautologies. This contains the decisive point. We have said that some things are arbitrary in the symbols that we use and that some things are not.[5] In logic it is only the latter that express: but that means that logic is not a field in which *we* express what we wish with the help of signs, but rather one in which the nature of the absolutely necessary signs speaks for itself. If we know the logical syntax of any sign-language, then we have already been given all the propositions of logic. (*TLP*, 6. 124)

This Realism is vestigial because it has abandoned nearly all the territory claimed by past Realists and retreated to a very restricted corner. Earlier in the *Tractatus* he had argued against Russell's more extensive Realism. Russell had included specific kinds of facts in his account of the ontological foundations of logic, and Wittgenstein ridiculed the idea that the world had to contain facts as complex as the structures explored by logic (*TLP*, 5.55–5.5571).

But what exactly did he take to be indicated about the world by the fact that certain combinations of symbols are tautologies? What he says is that it presupposes that names have meanings and elementary propositions sense. We know that he believed that this, in its turn, indicated that language and world share the same logically atomic structure (see *TLP*, 2.021–2.0211). So the match between language and reality that is presupposed by the emergence of tautologies is both profound and extensive. But, of course, it is something that can only be shown and can never be reported in factual language, because we have no way of indicating the independent character of the material that language was required to match. This is his explanation of the fact that the limit of language can be drawn only from within language (see Preface to the *Tractatus*, 3). The doctrine is clearly a kind of Realism and it may be called 'Vestigial Realism' to mark its minimalist character. It is this Vestigial Realism that was superseded by his later treatment of logical necessity.

---

[5] See *TLP*, 3.342.

It is not easy to describe the transition to his later treatment without exaggerating the distance from the starting line to the finishing line. The movement may look like a journey beginning with a pure Realism, which requires logically necessary propositions to correspond to independently discernible necessities in reality, and ending with a pure Conventionalism, which relies on a capricious Voluntarism. But, in fact, the distance between the start and the finish is not so great, and it will soon become apparent that both his treatments of logical necessity rely on the interplay between reality and our reactions to it. For his early theory, that the truths of logic are tautologies that show something about the world, still relies on a connection between reality and our reactions to it; and his later Voluntarism does not leave our reactions at the mercy of caprice.

The crucial point at which the two treatments diverge is his attitude to proof in logic, and if we want to understand the transition from the first to the second treatment, it is a good idea to start by following what theologians call the *Via Remotionis*—i.e., we should start by establishing what, according to him, proof in logic is *not* like and leave its positive characterization until later. What it is *not* like is the use of logical necessities to derive contingent conclusions from contingent premisses in daily life. That use of logical necessities leads to conclusions that can be confirmed by observation, but proof in logic does not have to submit its results to any similar test. We may say, if we like, that a valid theorem corresponds to a real necessity, but there is no test of the reality of the necessity that will serve as the counterpart of the verification of contingent conclusions proved by logic from contingent premisses. However, it does not follow that proof in logic is a speculative process, but only that logically necessary truths are not tested in anything like the way that contingent truths are tested. This is Wittgenstein's basic insight and it is common to both his treatments of logically necessary propositions.

In his early treatment, he dismisses proof in logic as an unnecessary pastime and relies, instead, on the test for tautology. As a matter of fact, this test works for the propositional calculus but cannot be extended to apply to all kinds of logical truth. Consequently, in his later work, he goes back to the question about the nature of proof in logic, and he comes to some surprising conclusions. The best way to understand these conclusions is to trace the lines of thought that led to them from the point at which he resumed philosophy in 1929.

The Vestigial Realism of the *Tractatus* was an elusive hypothesis. Instead of trying to specify what reality must be like if it is going to support logical necessities, it only requires it to have whatever characteristics are needed if names are to have meanings and elementary propositions sense. This reticence avoids the mistake of trying to give a specific description of reality in its raw, unassimilated, state. It is, therefore, not an example of pure Realism: the necessary characteristics of reality are specified only by their relation to language—they are whatever makes it possible for names to have meanings and elementary propositions sense.

This is certainly more explanatory than the bald assertion that logically necessary propositions must correspond to real necessities. For it tells us that they depend on a relation between language and reality and it tells us what effect that relation has on language. What it does not even try to explain is the emergence of new logical necessities. If that is not always the result of the discovery of new tautologies, a different kind of explanation was needed. That explanation was going to be provided by Wittgenstein's later treatment of proof in logic.

There was also another, deeper reason for his abandonment of Vestigial Realism when he resumed philosophy in 1929. Vestigial Realism assumed that the world must have some feature that facilitated the emergence of tautologies, but it did not specify what that feature was—it identified it only as whatever allowed names to have meanings and elementary propositions senses. However, this reticence did not protect Vestigial Realism from the objection that it still left necessary truths precariously dependent on contingencies—unspecified contingencies, but nevertheless contingencies (cf. *TLP*, 5.552, discussed above, p. 72).

When he resumed philosophy in 1929, he came to see that this was a fatal flaw in his earlier Vestigial Realism. It left it vulnerable to a simple but profound objection: logical necessities cannot depend on contingencies—not even on unspecified contingencies. For if the property of the world that facilitated the emergence of tautologies only belonged to it contingently, then it might never have belonged to it and in that case the tautologies would never have emerged: conversely, if tautologies have emerged, they cannot be based on a contingent, facilitating property of the world.

This criticism of his earlier Vestigial Realism is developed in *Philosophical Remarks*:

If I could describe the point of grammatical conventions by saying that they are made necessary by certain properties of the colours (say), then that would make the conventions superfluous, since in that case I would be able to say precisely that which the conventions exclude my saying. Conversely, if the conventions were necessary, i.e. if certain combinations of words had to be excluded as nonsensical, then for that very reason I cannot cite a property of colours that makes the connections necessary, since it would then be conceivable that the colours should not have this property and I could only express that by violating the conventions.    (*PR*, S 4)

The point is expressed more succinctly a little later:

... if anything is to count as nonsense in the grammar which is to be justified, then it cannot at the same time pass for sense in the grammar of the propositions that justify it (etc.).    (Ibid., S 7)

Evidently, the Vestigial Realism offered in the *Tractatus* was radically mistaken. The necessity of logical formulas was supposed to depend on a contingent situation, identified in a non-specific way, and both the existence and the non-existence of that situation were supposed to be presented in the same language. The failure of this explanation of logical necessities suggests an obvious remedy: we should seek the explanation in spontaneous but motivated developments *within* language.[6] This is the line of investigation that he began to follow in 1929 and it led to some surprising, but not necessarily discrediting, paradoxes. The clue that he followed in his investigation was not something theoretical, not a recondite feature of reality, but something that people require of logic in daily life, the reliable delivery of true conclusions from true premises. This shift from the metaphysical background to the practical foreground is, of course, characteristic of all his later philosophy.

His new line of investigation had another conspicuous advantage. Because it sought the origin of logically necessary truths in changes within language, it was not vulnerable to his criticism of his earlier Vestigial Realism. It did not have to use the same, unaltered language to present both the necessary truth and the contingent situation on which its emergence was supposed to depend. It could avoid this crippling limitation by always appealing to a change in language. In fact, there were two different kinds of change in language that he now invoked to explain the emergence of logically necessary truths. One involved an extended use of truth by definition, or analyticity; and the other relied on a rehabilitation of proof in logic. Both these changes were changes in the internal structure of language prompted by external experiential input (but not in the way that a child's first taste of a pineapple might prompt him to coin a new word for it (Hume's example) ).[7]

---

[6] An example of rational Voluntarism. See above, p. 66.
[7] See Hume, *Treatise of Human Nature*, Bk I, PI, S 1.

Wittgenstein's extension of the idea of truth by definition is a relatively simple matter.[8] Suppose that a substance that satisfies the existing definition of lead is discovered to have a specific gravity that approximates closely to a certain value. Then that value may be adopted as a further defining property of pure lead. If we want to understand the importance of this familiar Conventionalist move, we need to ask how it fares as a general explanation of certain logical necessities, and we need to see it against the background of the Vestigial Realism of the *Tractatus*, and to trace its emergence from the ashes of that theory.

The Vestigial Realism of the *Tractatus* had avoided the mistake of trying to give an independent characterization of the features of the world that facilitated the emergence of tautologies. It identified those features only as 'whatever made it possible for names to have meanings and elementary propositions sense'. But it still remained vulnerable to the criticism that a necessary truth cannot depend in this way on a contingency—not even on a non-specific contingency—and so it is incoherent to describe the dependence in a single, unchanged language. The only coherent way to develop this kind of theory is to suppose that there is a change in language made in response to a change in the world, which is described in the original, unchanged language.

It is crucially important that the change in language is not capricious but rationally motivated. People did not *have* to make the change and in that sense it was arbitrary, but it was not capricious, because there was a good reason for making it. In the example used so far, the fact that the substance had a specific gravity that always approximated to the same value made it convenient to include that value among its defining properties. This extension of the idea of truth by definition involves a theory about the packaging of information in propositions. The new way of packaging the information is more convenient, or perhaps only more vivid, as it is when we say 'it is going to rain' instead of using an inflected future tense, as Latin does. But whatever the precise motive for the new way of speaking, the situation that prompts us to adopt it is describable in the old way. It is crucially important that the innovation is motivated by a situation described in the old language. That condition was not met by the Vestigial Realism of the *Tractatus* (see above, p. 76).

---

[8] His development of the idea of the machine treated as a symbol of its own future performance develops the extension in a more complex way. See *PI* I, SS 191–5, discussed above, pp. 30–33.

It is met by the new account which is essentially an account of linguistic innovation.

Wittgenstein employs several powerful metaphors to present this idea. He says that the connection between the original concept and its new criteria is 'hardened into a rule' or 'petrified' (see *RFM* VI, 22). The proposition that expresses the new connection is like a new part of a bank of a river produced by the deposit of silt [*OC*, SS 93–105). Or, in the case of a mathematical rule, '+1', he says:

Thus the truth of the proposition, that $4 + 1 = 5$, is so to speak, *overdetermined.* Overdetermined by this, that the result of the operation is defined to be the criterion that this operation has been carried out.

The proposition rests on one too many feet to be an empirical proposition. It will be used as a determination of the concept 'applying the operation "+1" to 4'. For we now have a new way of judging whether someone has followed the rule.   (*RFM* VI, 16)

The new necessary truth is adopted arbitrarily but not capriciously because its adoption is preceded by a completely successful career as a contingent proposition.

In the *Tractatus* this way of dealing with those necessary truths that are not tautologies ran into a problem, which Wittgenstein shelved at the time and tried, but failed, to solve later. The problem is an interesting one because in 1929 his failure to solve it in a way that would preserve the logical atomism of the *Tractatus* led to his abandonment of that doctrine. In fact, it was the first part of the structure to crumble.

The theory of analyticity seeks to explain all necessary truths either as truths of logic or as statements reducible to truths of logic by a judicious use of definitions. The problem that Wittgenstein faced in 1929 was a problem about the second disjunct which relied on definitions. In cases where suitable definitions were available, the theory worked smoothly: aeroplanes by definition must have wings and rockets by definition must lack wings. So it is impossible for the two classes to overlap and the impossibility is guaranteed by the two definitions. In this kind of case the impossibility is generated *within* language.

However, the necessary incompatibility of two complementary colours, like red and green, cannot be explained in this way. For the two colour-words are indefinable and their meanings can be fixed only by their applications to things. That seems to leave open the possibility that it is the two colours themselves that produce the incompatibility, which would then have nothing to do with language.

This led Wittgenstein in 1929 to make his first recantation of a major thesis of the *Tractatus*. He no longer maintained that elementary propositions must be logically independent of one another. The property of being coloured is a determinable, and it evidently breaks down into a set of determinate properties, the specific colours, each of which is logically incompatible with any of the others. The further analysis that he had formerly supposed to be needed is not needed. For what is applied to reality like a ruler is not a solitary proposition ascribing a determinate colour to an object, but a determinate proposition together with the automatic negation of all the other determinate propositions, which are logically incompatible with it, and so are not applied to the object. This entire set of propositions is what is like a ruler [9] and the individual propositions are like its graduating lines. To ascribe one colour to an object is automatically to withhold all the other colours.

This still leaves the question about the source of the incompatibility of the determinate colours unanswered. Is it produced by our use of the colour-words or by the colours themselves? Is there even any way of answering this question, given that it cannot be decided entirely *within* language, as it is when it can be set out in ordinary analytic formula, like the formula that specifies the difference between an aeroplane and a rocket?

Wittgenstein returned to these questions later in his life. In a long and difficult discussion of the incompatibility of two complementary colours he says

354 I want to say that there is a geometrical gap, not a physical one, between green and red.
355 But doesn't anything physical correspond to it? I do not deny that ... (Zettel, S 354–5)

What he denies is that the physical facts provide the whole explanation of the incompatibility. His idea seems to be that the words in which we record the incompatibility make an essential contribution to its existence. But how can they do that? Surely the two colours must already be incompatible: otherwise, it would be the assertion of their incompatibility that made them incompatible, and so it would be a premature assertion.[10]

---

[9] See *Yardstick and System of Propositions*, taken from Waismann's notes of conversations with Wittgenstein between December 1929 and September 1931 and published as Appendix 2 of *Philosophical Remarks*.

[10] See Ch. 2, pp. 26–27, for the discussion of a similar problem about linguistic regularity. How can an innovative application of a general word to a particular thing

He continues:

356 ... But what is the right simile here? That of a road that is physically impassable, or of the non-existence of a road? I.e. is it one of physical or mathematical impossibility?
357 We have a colour system as we have a number system. Do the systems reside in *our* nature or in the nature of things? How are we to put it? *Not* in the nature of numbers or colours.
358 Then is there something arbitrary about this system? Yes and no. It is akin both to what is arbitrary and to what is non-arbitrary.   (Zettel, SS 356–8)

This is a heavily qualified development of a much earlier verdict:

To a necessity in the world there corresponds an arbitrary rule in language. (*Cambridge Lectures*, 1931–1932, 57)

The verdict is expressed more explicitly later:

The only correlate in language to an intrinsic necessity is an arbitrary rule. It is the only thing that one can draw off[11] from this intrinsic necessity into a proposition.   (*Philosophical Grammar*, S 133)

The discussion in Zettel ends enigmatically:

... but has nature nothing to say here?
Indeed she has—but she makes herself audible in another way.
'You'll surely run up against existence and non-existence somewhere!' But that means against *facts*, not concepts.   (Zettel, S 364)

These texts convey a very convoluted message. What is clear is that he is rejecting the Realist's thesis that what makes this proposition logically necessary is any kind of correspondence with anything independently necessary in the world. If we look for anything of that kind in the world, we shall only find facts rather than necessities. But it is less clear what he is proposing as an alternative to Realism. These texts might be expected to reveal some connection between linguistic regularity and logical necessity. For example, the message might be that what ensures that the two colours do not overlap is simply the divergence of the techniques of applying the words 'red' and 'green'. But then we might still want to know whether this divergence is produced by

---

both modify its meaning and at the same time use its modified meaning to make a true statement about the thing? Surely, the two opposed directions of fit are exclusive alternatives? But, mysteriously, the facts ignore this objection.

[11] The translation of the German 'abziehen', 'milk out of', has been slightly altered.

the natures of the two sets of things *before* they were picked out by the two words or is only produced by the exercise of the techniques of applying the two words when we do pick them out. (Cf. Berkeley's argument that the attempt to think of an object with no connection with any mind is necessarily self-frustrating. (*Principles of Human Knowledge*, S XXIII).)

However, though this might seem to be a way of distinguishing two alternative explanations of these cases of incompatibility and adjudicating between them, it does not really succeed in doing so. For what could it mean to say that the two sets of things necessarily failed to overlap *before* the two words were applied to them? *Which* two sets of things? They must be specified and the two words must already be involved even if only in the formulation of the problem. So, inevitably, the question recurs: Is it only their involvement that produces the incompatibility, or was it always there? The investigation of this case seems to have led us into a wilderness where there are no answers.

The source of this problem is more evident than its solution. We are asking the Realist to identify two complementary colours in ways that do not even depend implicitly on our colour-vocabulary. If he names the two colours 'red' and 'green', we object that he is not doing what we asked him to do. He may then protest that he is using the two words as a temporary device to indicate the two colours that he means, and once we have understood which two colours he means, we can dispense with his method of identifying them, in much the same way that builders take down the scaffolding after the completion of a building. His point is that *those* two colours cannot overlap.

Our reply to this ought to be that it is not enough to point to two coloured objects, because isolated ostensive definitions do not give us the extension of the two colour-words, which he is now trying to avoid using.[12] So if he withdraws his original use of the two colour-words to make his references, he has not said anything: and if he retains it, the necessary incompatibility of the two colours may simply be a consequence of his use of that part of our colour-vocabulary. He cannot say anything without actually saying it. No doubt, the air is filled with unformulated necessary propositions, but it is only after they have been formulated that the source of their necessity—language or the world—can be investigated.[13]

---

[12] See above, pp. 79–80.
[13] Cf. *The Brown Book*, 158 ff. on the evasive use of the phrase 'a particular x'.

However, it must not be forgotten that the outcome might be that the source of the necessity does not lie exclusively with either of the two contestants, but only with their interaction at the interface between language and the world. It may be true that exclusive reliance on intra-linguistic considerations produces a convincing explanation of most necessary truths. But it does not follow that when we are forced to take into account what happens at the interface between language and the world—as we seem to be in this case—we forfeit the right to claim that the source of the necessity is linguistic. After all, a theory of meaning that omitted the relations established at the interface would be incomplete (see *PI* I, S 201) and the fact that those relations connect words with things is not enough to show that the resultant necessities are not linguistic.

Wittgenstein's extended use of truth by definition was not the only line of thought that led him from his earlier Vestigial Realism to his later Voluntarism and Conventionalism. The development of his new ideas about logical necessity also owed much to his rehabilitation of proof in logic. It was a highly qualified rehabilitation which did not go far enough to satisfy most Realists, but it did give proof in logic a more important role than he had given it in the *Tractatus*: he now conceded that it generated new principles of inference for us to 'put in the archive'[14] for future use outside logic when we infer contingent conclusions from contingent premisses. However, this concession to proof in logic fell far short of the Realist's estimate of its importance and most of the criticism of his later treatment of logical necessity is aimed at his later treatment of proof in logic.

The convergence of criticism on this point is understandable. Few people object to the idea that the acceptance of a truth by definition is an act of will that is not forced on us, but it really is highly paradoxical to suggest that the conclusion of a proof in logic is something that we do not have to accept. So the conflict between Wittgenstein and the Realist becomes very heated at this point, and there is a real risk that it may produce a kind of melt-down of the ideas that gave rise to it. So it is a good policy to enter this controversy cautiously by first identifying some points that are, and ought to remain, fixed.

The first point that is often forgotten in the heat of battle is that correspondence with a real necessity is not the only test of the acceptability of a truth of logic. Since truths of logic are used outside

---

14  See *RFM* III, 29–31.

logic to deduce contingent conclusions from contingent premisses, their success in achieving that result is available as another test of their acceptability. It is also a test that yields an independently identifiable result, unlike the test of correspondence with a real necessity (cf. the emptiness of the Realist's invocation of universals to explain the regular application of general words see above, p. 17).

It is also worth remembering that it was characteristic of Wittgenstein's thinking to seek the test of the acceptability of truths of logic in something accessible to ordinary people in daily life (see above, p. 68 ff.). It is a mistake to assume that the only objective test of a truth of logic is to investigate whether it corresponds to a real necessity. That description is like the kind of description of a research project that might be pinned to the door of a laboratory rather than a description of the method followed by the investigators inside. So right at the start of this controversy the lines of battle have been drawn up erroneously. The test that the Realist treats as inadequate may be more real than the test that he wants to substitute for it.

Logically necessary propositions are demonstrations of correct grammar, and soon after his resumption of philosophy in 1929 Wittgenstein makes the point that grammar

cannot be justified [namely, by a Realist demonstration of its correspondence with an independent reality] But it is not arbitrary in so far as it is not arbitrary what rules of grammar I can make use of. Grammar described by itself is arbitrary; what makes it not arbitrary is its use. (*CLI*, 49)

The history of geometry provides convincing examples of the interplay between the axiomatization of different systems and their applications. In the history of logic, the examples are fewer and less convincing and we shall need to inquire later why this is so and whether it reveals a weakness in Wittgenstein's combination of Voluntarism and Conventionalism.

It is extraordinarily difficult to keep a level head when one tries to answer the question whether Wittgenstein's later account of logical necessity is acceptable. We reflect that a logically valid argument has to move on the track of a real necessity, and, because we are dazzled by the way in which singular factual propositions achieve truth, we find it overwhelmingly natural to say that logically necessary propositions have to correspond to real necessities. We think that if there were no real necessities to which logically necessary propositions could correspond, they could only be based on Humpty-Dumpty's non-rational Voluntarism (see above, p. 25). Anxiety takes over at this point and we feel that it would be outrageous to turn free will loose in the field of rationality.[15] We forget that the criterion of general necessary truth does not have to be at all like the criterion of singular contingent truth, and so we pass over the obvious candidate—the reliable delivery of true contingent conclusions from true contingent premisses—and we reassure ourselves with the empty formula 'correspondence with a real necessity'. When the rational Voluntarism that lies behind Wittgenstein's Conventionalism is presented without any mention of the obvious candidate for the post of criterion, our choice of principles to be included in 'the archive' for future use will seem entirely capricious, and so we look for another criterion and look in the wrong direction for it.

It is a good policy to open the discussion of this controversy by considering two texts that exhibit the disposition of forces on the battlefield. One is the passage from *Cambridge Lectures 1929–1932*, which has just been quoted (see above, p. 83). The other is a later text in *Remarks on the Foundations of Mathematics* that has yet to be quoted (see below, pp. 85–86).

In the earlier text he concedes that grammar described by itself is arbitrary. But he claims that 'it is not arbitrary in so far as it is not arbitrary what rules of grammar I can make use of'. If a network of logical inferences can be developed and applied to the world with true results, what more can we ask of it? When a system of thought has achieved a fit with the world in this way, it is not necessary to look for another simpler kind of fit modelled on the correspondence with the world achieved by singular factual sentences.

The task of constructing the system is ours, and it is only after we have completed it that we can use it to produce a description of the world that inspired it. When we feel moved to add something new to the system, we do not act capriciously. But the guidance that we receive is not like the discovery of a possible possibility waiting to be recognized as a real possibility. There is no chart of the space of possibilities that have not yet been specified in language. This is the feature of the limit of language that is emphasized in the Preface to the *Tractatus* (*TLP*, 3; see below, p. 94). So, though we may picture the domain of facts as a sphere contained within a larger sphere of unrealized possibilities, we cannot picture that sphere within an even larger sphere of possible possibilities.

---

[15] This was the complaint made by contemporary and later critics of Descartes's Voluntarism. But freedom of the will is compatible with rationality of decision.

This limit to the pictorial resources of nested spheres is connected with Wittgenstein's move from Vestigial Realism to his later combination of Voluntarism and Conventionalism. His final criticism of the Vestigial Realism of the *Tractatus* was that logical necessities cannot depend on contingencies in the world—not even on very non-specific contingencies—and, anyway, it was a mistake to express in the same language both the necessary truth and the contingent facts on which it was supposed to depend (see above, p. 75).

That mistaken inclusion of both items in what can be expressed in a single language is corrected in his later treatment of logical necessity. For, as will soon become apparent, the new treatment separates two distinct phases in the emergence of a new truth of logic. First, there is the old language in which the reasons for acknowledging the new logical truth in language are set out in detail; and then the new logical truth is acknowledged in what is, as a result, a new and different language.[16] His old idea was that logical necessities depend on certain very general facts about the world. His new idea was that contingent facts do have a role to play in the emergence of logical necessities, but only because they suggest the adoption of new criteria for words already in use or the introduction of new patterns of inference that were already implicit in existing patterns.

The second text which will serve to set the stage for this stubborn controversy belongs to Part I of *Remarks on the Foundations of Mathematics*, which was written about ten years later than the first text:

'Then according to you everybody could continue the series as he likes; and so infer *anyhow*.'[17] In that case we shan't call it 'continuing the series' and presumably not 'inference'. And thinking and inferring (like counting) is, of course, bounded for us, not by an arbitrary definition, but by the natural limits corresponding to the body of what can be called the role of thinking in our lives.

For we are at one over this, that the laws of inference do not compel him [i.e. namely, the maverick] to say or to write such and such like rails compelling a locomotive. And if you say that, while he may indeed *say* it, still he can't *think*

---

[16] This movement from the Vestigial Realism of the *Tractatus* to the later combination of Conventionalism and Voluntarism might seem to support the New Wittgensteinians' contention that he formulated his early doctrine of showing 'with his tongue in his cheek'. But does it not look as if he simply changed his mind when he moved from the Vestigial Realism of the *Tractatus* to his later account of logical necessity? Why credit him with prescience? (See I. Proops, 'The New Wittgenstein: A Critique', *European Journal of Philosophy* (December 2001), and see above, p. 32 n. 5.)

[17] Wittgenstein puts this first sentence into the mouth of a critic.

it, then I am only saying that that means, not; try as he may he can't think it, but: it is for us an essential part of thinking that—in talking, writing, etc.—he makes *this sort* of transition. And I say further that the line between what we include in 'thinking' is no more a hard and fast one than the line between what is still and what is no longer called 'regularity'.   (*RFM* I, 116)

These two texts make his Conventionalism (and Voluntarism) sound very reasonable and easy to accept. The adoption and use of the theorems in a logical calculus is not capricious but based on an objective test: we find that we can use them—presumably by making inferences outside logic and finding that they always deliver true conclusions from true premises. So proof in logic provides us with the tools that we need in daily life for proving contingent conclusions from contingent premises and is a kind of machine for producing lesser machines for daily use. When a theorem is proved, 'We put it in the archive' for future use outside logic (*RFM* III, 29–31). This concedes more importance to proof in logic than he had allowed it in the *Tractatus*. It is also a clear example of his policy of building up a linguistic system from its foundations in our ordinary thinking.

The second text also makes another very persuasive point: the line between what counts and what does not count as thinking is not a hard and fast line, and in this it is like the line between what counts and what does not count as the regular application of words to things. That is yet another feature that allowed him to use his treatment of that topic as a model for his treatment of logical inference.

However, when he is discussing inferences in detail, what he says often sounds very paradoxical. Here is what is perhaps the most extreme example:

'But am I not compelled, then, to go the way I do in a chain of inferences?'—Compelled? After all, I can presumably go as I choose! 'But if you want to remain in accord with the rules, you *must* go this way.'—Not at all, I call *this* accord.—'Then you have changed the meaning of the word "accord" or the meaning of the rule'.—No; 'Who says what "change" and "remaining the same" mean here?'

However many rules you give me, I give a rule which justifies *my* employment of your rules.   (*RFM* I, 113)

This startling text takes Wittgenstein's reliance on incompletely formulatable techniques for the application of general words and extends it to a new area, the making of logical inferences. If we look back at his earlier discussions of linguistic regularity, we can see that what he says here belongs to the tradition of Cartesian Voluntarism rather than to the Humean tradition of passive, but inevitable, acceptance. I may feel compelled to follow a rule of inference that I understand and accept, but that is not like the compulsion that keeps a locomotive on the rails.

No. And it is also unlike the compulsion to call this flower blue when calling it that would be the natural way to continue the application of the word 'blue'. In both these cases the compulsion is the consequence of a general policy which I have adopted voluntarily when I could have adopted a different general policy. When I invested in linguistic regularity, the dividend was the discovery of natural regularities in the world around me (see above, p. 20), and now my investment in logical necessity yields a bonus on the dividend. The similarity between this case and the case of inference is impressive, and it is the force that drives this part—the central part—of Wittgenstein's later philosophy of language.

The immediate effect of this explanation is to reduce the paradoxical character of the startling text which implies that it is up to me whether I choose to follow an ordinary chain of inferences in the customary way, whereas it is not up to the locomotive to choose to stay on the rails. We may call this 'the minimal point' of the startling text, and it is a point that is both valid and important. The compulsion that I feel when I follow a chain of inferences in the normal way is self-imposed and so reconcilable with Voluntarism. It is not like the compulsion that keeps a locomotive on the rails.

There can be no doubt that in this text Wittgenstein is, at least, making the minimal point. His explanation of his refusal to agree that the compulsion that I feel is absolute and unconditional makes that clear. He says that I am simply taking for granted the meaning of the rule that I am following, or taking for granted the meaning of 'accord with the rule'. This is clearly an application of the point made in *PI* I, S 201:

This was our paradox: no course of action could be determined by a rule, because every course of action can be made out to accord with the rule. The answer was: if everything can be made out to accord with the rule, then it can also be made out to conflict with it. And so there would be neither accord nor conflict here. (*P.I.* I, S 201, discussed above p. 18 ff.)

So in the startling text just quoted from *Remarks on the Foundations of Mathematics*, he is, at least, making the minimal point, that the compulsion that I feel when I follow a chain of inferences in the normal way is self-imposed and so reconcilable with Voluntarism.

But is he also making the further point, that it would be possible to imagine that someone might adopt an alternative to our normal way of following a chain of inferences and still make some kind of success of it? We may call an affirmative answer to this question 'the maximal point'. So, granted that he is, at least, making the minimal point, the further question is whether he is also making the maximal point.

The answer to this question lies in a penumbra on the boundary of his explicit later philosophical method. It is true that the maximal point would give convincing substance to his idea that the concept of *thinking* has shifting limits. He could say that logic is like geometry, where we have a choice between different systems that can be applied successfully in different areas—Euclidean geometry in local space and Riemannian geometry in interstellar space.[18] It must be admitted that if there are similar examples in logic, they are less spectacular. But why would it not be enough for him to make the less dramatic point that it is we who apply the principles of logic to our thinking, even though there is no alternative reliable way of extracting true conclusions from true premisses. Voluntarism might still give the right explanation of Hobson's choice. ('You can have this horse or you can walk'). Even madness has its styles of thinking. But there is no clear answer to the question whether Wittgenstein in this text is restricting his defence of Voluntarism to the minimal point, or extending it to include some version of the maximal point.[19]

However, even if he is confining himself to the minimal point, that would be enough to reduce the paradoxical character of the startling text. If someone accepts the premisses but withholds his assent from

[18] See Robertson, 'Geometry as a "Branch of Physics"', in *The Philosophy of Albert Einstein* P. A. Schilpp (ed.), Library of Living Philosophers (Evanston, Ill., 1949).

[19] There are other texts in which he clearly does make the maximal point and the most audacious one sketches a bizarre way of calculating the amount of wood in a pile (*RFM* I, SS 143–52). However, that is an example of bizarre mathematical calculation rather than bizarre logical inference. Dummett complains that all such examples are thin and unconvincing, 'Wittgenstein's Philosophy of Mathematics', *Philosophical Review*, (1968), 324–48 but Stroud argues that this is only because we cannot fully understand procedures that are so different from our own 'Wittgenstein and Logical Necessity', *Philosophical Review* (1974), 504–18. However, a large part of the explanation may only be that Wittgenstein's Voluntarism did not need to include the maximal point and that is why he only sketched it in perfunctorily. So in the startling text what he emphasizes is the connection between the feeling of compulsion and the acceptance of a rule and that point—the minimal point—would retain its importance even in cases where it would be hard to imagine a plausible alternative to the rule that we now find acceptable.

the conclusion of a logically valid inference, he presumably does so for a reason and not out of pure caprice. He would not be taking his cue from Humpty-Dumpty and saying 'these are my premises and I can do what I like with them.' Wittgenstein is suggesting that he is withholding his assent from the conclusion *only because* he does not think that the usual conception of validity is convincing, and not in *spite of* finding it sufficiently convincing in general but flouting it in this particular case. It is very important that this recusant is not exhibiting indiscriminate cussedness: he is making the reasonable point, that we do not experience logical necessity as a bolt from the blue but only in the nexus of a rule of inference. It is equally important that the recusant pays absolutely no attention to the fact that we have a way of distinguishing acceptable from unacceptable rules of inference: the rules that we adopt always lead us from true premises to true conclusions. It must not be forgotten that this is an *objective* criterion which has as good a claim to be a Realist's criterion as correspondence to a logical necessity (see above, p. 76).

No doubt, Realists will refuse to admit that the consistent delivery of true conclusions from true premises really is as good a criterion of the acceptability of a rule of inference as correspondence to a logical necessity. When Wittgenstein points out that 'correspondence to a logical necessity' is an empty phrase, like 'correspondence to a universal' in the controversy about the application of a general word,[20] Realists will counter-attack by pointing out that contingent general propositions, too, have to satisfy Wittgenstein's criterion, and so it fails to isolate the distinctive character of logically necessary propositions.

This takes us to the heart of the matter. Wittgenstein will meet this counter-attack by claiming that there is never any extra element of necessity in the regular sequences that nature provides for our exploitation or enjoyment. The necessity lies in our reactions, which have just as much right to be represented in our language *in the same breath* as the stimuli that caused them. This, of course, is only a preliminary move in the controversy between Wittgenstein and Realists, and he still has to distinguish logically necessary from nomologically necessary propositions. His idea must be that this distinction depends on an *extra* contribution made by the speakers of the language. Logical necessity is generated by what he calls 'petrifaction'. The connection is included in the meaning of the word that designates the first member of

---

[20] See above, p. 67.

the connected couple, and so what had been a mobile joint is fossilized in the record.[21]

Petrifaction produced by the extended use of truth by definition was only one of Wittgenstein's two ways of explaining the origin of necessary truths, and it was discussed above (p. 77 ff.). The other way of explaining the origin of necessary truths was proof in logic and that still remains to be discussed.

His new conception of proof in logic is closely connected with his other major innovation, the extended use of the idea of truth by definition. In that case necessities that would have floated mysteriously between language and reality were tied down and domesticated within language. Similarly, proof in logic, which might seem to be a way of discovering necessities deeply embedded in reality, was really only a device that revealed connections between different patterns in our own thought and language. Or perhaps this way of describing the similarity between the two innovations owes too much to the old way of distinguishing objectivity from subjectivity. His real aim was to re-work that distinction by equating objectivity with controlled subjectivity. His success, if he did succeed, depends on the nature of the control.

When he extended the use of truth by definition, he relied on a very perspicuous use of his concept of 'petrifaction'. In that case the physical world is in control, and we merely substitute a perfect, internally generated necessity for an apparently perfect, but necessarily precarious, externally generated necessity. His new treatment of proof in logic, which is a partial rehabilitation of it after his earlier demotion of it in the *Tractatus*, has a different structure. The dominant concept is what he calls 'the archive'—i.e., our set of rules of inference already in use in daily life. Proof in logic takes some of these rules, expresses them as theorems, and deduces from them further theorems to be included in the 'archive' and used by us as rules of inference in daily life. His idea in this case is that we see that the new rule of inference is equivalent to the combination of the original rules and so we can use it with the same confidence that we used them. You see that you would be doing the same thing that you were doing when you followed the original rules separately as distinct steps.[22]

This way of looking at proof in logic relies heavily on perspicuity. You see that if you can use the rules that are formulated as premisses, then

---

[21] See above, p. 78 ff.
[22] See C. Diamond, 'The Realistic Spirit', ch. 9, *The Face of Necessity* (MIT Press, 1991).

you can just as well use the new rule that emerges as the conclusion. A logical calculus is a kind of factory which makes the tools that we use in inferences in daily life. The reliance on perspicuity is probably a remote effect of the influence of Schopenhauer (see above, p. 68 ff.) and it might be thought to make proof in logic an excessively subjective procedure. But there is an objective test of the tools in their use in daily life—they must always deliver true contingent conclusions from true contingent premisses.

When Wittgenstein's critics claim that his new treatment of proof in logic makes it an excessively subjective procedure, they are testing it against the vague traditional distinction between subjective and objective. That distinction takes its start from the separation of what is contributed to perception by the object and what is contributed by the perceiving subject. But Wittgenstein identified the objective with what is intersubjectively agreed.[23] That might make him look like an idealist, until we remember that the agreement is not *about* thought or language, but *in* thought and language and *about* the world. It is agreement in a way of thinking about the world, and before a particular way of thinking about it emerged there would be no point onto which the question about the nature of Reality could be focused. On the other hand, after a particular way of thinking about it had emerged—our way, for example—though there would now be a point onto which the question could be focused, the answer would inevitably be disappointing: 'Just try to understand the structure of our way of thinking about the world and the junctures at which it might have developed in different ways and why it did not develop in different ways. That is all that you can do. There is no fulcrum for Archimedes' lever'.

There are several points at which this rather bleak philosophy is easily misunderstood. First, it is traditionally classified as Conventionalism and that is an inadequate label. Second, it seems to give a sadly deflated account of logical necessity—can that really be all there is to it? Third, we tend to think of research in logic as exploration and of proof in logic as discovery of necessary truth, and Wittgenstein's treatment does less than justice to these natural tendencies. These points will be taken up and discussed in the remainder of this chapter.

Something has already been said about the shortfall of the label 'Conventionalism' (see above, p. 66 ff.). It is apt to suggest a conference at

---

[23] See *PI* I, SS 240–2.

which agreement is reached about the criterion of a scientific term—for example, agreement on the requirement that pure lead must have a certain specific gravity. It also suggests capriciousness because Wittgenstein often says that the decision that is reached is arbitrary and that word is often used with the implication that the decision was needed only as a matter of convenience and not because there was a reason for reaching that particular decision rather than some other decision. Moreover, the label 'Conventionalism' under-emphasizes the important fact that deciding is as much a function of the will as a function of the intellect. That was the point on which earlier critics of Voluntarism felt misgivings: surely it is risky to turn the will loose in the field of rationality. No doubt, we are not guided by rational principles in the same kind of way that a locomotive is guided by the rails on which it runs: we have to decide—it does not—and we decide not by taking an oath of conformity but simply by taking part in discussions that meet those standards. But the really important point is that even in this rarefied atmosphere our decisions can be rational and Wittgenstein gives the reasons for them.

This is part of the answer to a question that was posed earlier (see above, p. 67): 'Is Wittgenstein basing agreement in judgements and rational procedures on historical anthropology or on logical analysis?' The answer is 'neither, he bases them on an ongoing, mainly voluntary conformity to the rules of one of the most important procedures that there are for children to learn—speaking a language—and not just a language for expressing thoughts that they already have, but a language embodying principles that will carry them on more distant flights.

The second objection to Wittgenstein's treatment of logical necessity was that it is sadly deflationary and reduces the grandeur of the discipline to something very ordinary. This might be used as an objection to much of his later philosophy. But is deflation really a fault? He certainly did not think so. For when he is describing the transition from the philosophy of the *Tractatus* to his later philosophy, he says:

We are under the illusion that what is peculiar, profound, essential, in our investigation, resides in its trying to grasp the incomparable essence of language. That is, the order existing between the concepts of proposition, word, proof, truth, experience and so on. This order is a *super*-order between—so to speak—*super*-concepts. Whereas, of course, if the words 'language', 'experience', 'world', have a use, it must be as humble a one as that of the words, 'table', 'lamp', 'door'.   (*PI* I, S 97)

If we ask which of the two Wittgensteinian innovations that have been discussed in this chapter is the more mundane, the answer is undoubtedly his extended use of truth by definition. That, as has already been remarked, is merely an example of a change in the packaging of information in a sentence: a predicate that had been treated as only contingently connected with the subject is now treated as a criterion of the application of the subject-term. What could be simpler? However, in his discussion of the machine taken as a symbol of its own future performance, the use that he makes of this shift of information is far from simple (see above, p. 30 ff.).

What makes his extended use of truth by definition important is our tendency to run the two kinds of necessity together and so to generate the fantasy that there is a third kind that will combine the absolute certainty of definitional necessity with the informativeness of inductively established necessity. So when he applies the distinction to the experience of grasping the meaning of a word in a flash he says

'It's as if we could grasp the whole use of the word in a flash'. Like *what* e.g?—Can't the use—in a certain sense—be grasped in a flash? And in *what* sense can it not?—The point is that it is as if we could 'grasp it in a flash' in another and much more direct sense than that.—But have you a model for this? No, it is just that this expression suggests itself to us. As the result of the crossing of different pictures.

You have no model of this superlative fact, but you are seduced into using a super-expression. (It might be called a philosophical superlative.)   (*PI* I, SS 191–2, quoted above, pp. 30–31)

The corrective is to realize that absolute certainty is attainable only by basing it on truth by definition. This topic is developed in detail in *Lectures on the Philosophy of Mathematics*, pp. 196–9 and *Remarks on the Foundations of Mathematics* I, SS 118–27.

The third objection to Wittgenstein's account of logical necessity was that it does less than justice to our natural tendency to think of research in logic as exploration and of proof in logic as the discovery of necessary truths. But what would justice be in this case?

We may set the stage for answering this question by citing three propositions from the *Tractatus*:

It will therefore only be in language that the limit can be drawn.   (*TLP*, Preface, 3)

My fundamental idea is that the 'logical constants' are not representatives; there can be no representation of the logic of facts.   (*TLP*, 4.0312)

We can foresee only what we ourselves construct.   (*TLP*, 5–556)

It would be easy to suppose that the last of these three propositions belongs to his later philosophy, because it is a perfect expression of his Conventionalism and Voluntarism. In fact, it is the early point of growth from which his later treatment of logic emerged and expanded. It occurs in a passage in the *Tractatus* in which he is criticizing Russell for allowing logic to depend on certain general facts about the structure of the world. The premiss from which he derives his criticism is that

Logic is *prior* to every experience that something *is so*.
   It is prior to the question 'How?', not prior to the question 'What?'.   (*TLP*, 5.552, quoted above, p. 72)

That is why the Realism of the *Tractatus* can only be vestigial, and even in that form cannot survive for long, and why the idea, that logical connectives function in the same way as names, is absurd (see *TLP*, 4.0312).

The proposition quoted from the Preface to the *Tractatus* is as important in his later philosophy as it is in his early philosophy. We establish facts by discovering that possibilities are realized, but we do not establish possibilities by discovering that possibilities of possibilities are realized. If a sentence lacks sense, we can often give it a sense by relating it to other sentences that already have a sense. But we do not have to explore an outer ring of possibilities of possibility in order to discover which of them are real possibilities. That is part of the point of Wittgenstein's policy of building up language and logic from the level of their daily use. We may picture facts as a sphere floating in a space of possibilities, but we must not use the same image again to illustrate the relation between real possibilities and possible possibilities. It would be better to say that the sphere of facts produces, or, at least, shapes in an Einsteinian way, the space in which it floats.[24]

But these are only pictures. The plain truth of the matter is that the innovative expansions of language that Wittgenstein discusses in his treatment of logical necessity all start within language. They start with a well-confirmed general statement which almost asks to be guaranteed by definition, or with the premisses of a proof in logic in which the conclusion can be foreseen before it is drawn. So the innovation is a step that is made almost inevitable by the momentum of the thought behind

[24] See above, pp. 71 n. 3 and 84.

it, and not by the instrinsic attractiveness of real possibilities waiting for recognition in the limbo of possible possibilities.

The thing that's so difficult to understand can be expressed like this. *As long as we remain in the province of the true-false games, a change in the grammar can only lead us from* one *such game to another, and never from something true to something false. On the other hand, if we go outside the province of these games, we don't any longer call it 'language' and 'grammar', and once again we don't come into contradiction with reality.*   (*PG*, S 68)

# 5

# Ego

'I', or if we prefer to give it the *gravitas* of Latin, 'Ego', is a surprisingly elusive concept, and Wittgenstein's concern with the problems that it presents to a philosopher emerges very early in his writings.

The I, the I, that is what is deeply mysterious. (*NB 1914–1916*, 5/8/16)

His treatment of the concept leads him into two paradoxes, one of which occurs in the *Tractatus*, while the other is developed in his later writings. Both can be stated concisely.

The first paradox is formulated in the discussion of solipsism in the *Tractatus*:

5.6 *The limits of my language* mean the limits of my world.
5.61 Logic pervades the world: the limits of the world are also its limits.
  So we cannot say in logic, 'The world has this in it, and this, but not that.'
  For that would appear to presuppose that we were excluding certain possibilities, and that cannot be the case, since it would require that logic should go beyond the limits of the world; for only in that way could it view these limits from the other side as well.
  We cannot think what we cannot think: so what we cannot think we cannot *say* either.
5.62 This remark provides the key to the problem, how much truth there is in solipsism.
  For what the solipsist *means* is quite correct: only it cannot be *said*, but makes itself manifest.
  The world is *my* world: this is manifest in the fact that the limits of *language* (of that language which alone I understand) mean the limits of *my world*.

This is paradoxical, because one would not expect solipsism to contain any truth and perhaps least of all a truth about language. For the truth of 'I alone exist' would exclude the possibility of finding any conclusive evidence for its truth.

The second paradox does not—at least, on the face of it—involve any philosophical theory. It is the simple claim that the pronoun 'I' does not make a reference. This claim is made in *The Blue Book* (1933–1934):

'To say "I have pain" is no more a statement *about* a particular person than moaning is. 'But surely the word "I" in the mouth of a man refers to the man who says it: it points to himself, and very often a man who says it actually points to himself with his finger.' But it was quite superfluous to point to himself. He might just as well only have raised his hand.' (*The Blue Book*, 66–7)

Two years later in *Notes for Lectures*, he wrote:

The word 'I' does not designate a person  (*Ludwig Wittgenstein: Philosophical Occasions 1912–1951*, ed. J. Klagge and A. Nordmann, 228)

This remark is repeated in MS 116, p. 218.

This too is paradoxical, but not for a reason that depends on any philosophical theory. A person's name is used to refer to that person and a personal pronoun takes over the function of the name, and so can stand alone in a sentence, making the same reference. There is a sharp contrast here between a personal pronoun and a relative pronoun, which cannot stand alone and make reference, but has to derive its reference from the antecedent name of the person and make it anaphorically with the help of the name. These are just grammatical facts.

So the two paradoxes have very different characters. One is constructed on the high ground of philosophical theory, while the other seems to develop out of the ordinary exigencies of communication between people. This difference is a typical manifestation of the general difference between Wittgenstein's philosophy before and after 1929.

The paradoxical assessment of solipsism is based on a very sophisticated interpretation of the solipsist's thesis. His basic claim is that 'Only I exist'—*Solus ipse*. What we would like to be able to ask him is, 'Where do you draw the line between what is you and what is not you?' It is, of course, going to be a special kind of boundary, because it will not divide existing things into two groups, like a river running through a forest. That point about the limit of language was made in the Preface to the *Tractatus*:

Thus the aim of the book is to draw a limit to thought, or rather—not to thought but to the expression of thoughts: for in order to be able to draw a limit to thought, we should have to find both sides of the limit thinkable (i.e., we should have to be able to think what cannot be thought).

It will therefore only be in language that the limit can be drawn, and what lies on the other side of the limit will simply be nonsense.  (*TLP*, 3)

In this explanation of the aim of his book, Wittgenstein is assuming that his pictorial theory of sentences is essentially correct: genuine thoughts, like genuine sentences, owe their senses to one-to-one correlations of their components with objects. This assumption enables him to move to and fro between sentences with senses and names of existing objects: the solipsist draws a limit to the former by drawing a limit to the latter. It is in this way that his solipsism acquires a linguistic character: he draws a line around existing objects and by so doing draws a line around sentences with senses.

Both boundaries have the same peculiar character. They do not divide things into two groups—on one side of the boundary objects that exist and on the other side objects that do not exist, or, equivalently, on one side of the boundary sentences that make sense and on the other side sentences that do not make sense. For the solipsist's idea is that he stands on one side of the boundary among the things that exist using sentences with senses, while on the other side of it there is only a void.[1]

## THE FIRST PARADOX

The solipsist praised by Wittgenstein for his insight in the Preface to the *Tractatus* is a linguistic solipsist. The question that we would all like to be able to put to him is, 'How do you draw the line between what is you and what is not you?' Do you exclude from your list of existing things everything that is supposed to lie outside your mind? But would that not make you like a cartographer who claimed that the only reality lay within his maps—a character who might figure in one of Borges stories?

But this question underestimates the complexity of Wittgenstein's position. His linguistic solipsist can certainly tell us how he saw the world *before* his conversion to his theory: there were two distinct sets of things and he drew a line between them and labelled one of them 'self' and the other 'not-self'. But after his conversion he had no use for the label 'not-self', because there was no longer anything to which he could apply it. That forced him to take a different view of the line that he had drawn. For he had to avoid the mistake of the lady who is reported to have said to Russell, after he had given a lecture: 'I'm so happy to find

---

[1] Or, better, only a vacuum. See p. 71, n. 3.

that you too are a solipsist. I've been one all my life and I've always been surprised that there aren't more of us.'

Such social chatter is obviously superficial. For the line drawn by the linguistic solipsist is not primarily a line that separates true from false existential sentences, nor even significant from senseless existential sentences. The sentences that the linguistic solipsist is trying to capture within his boundary are essentially those that he himself finds intelligible, and the connection with existence is then a consequence of the theory of meaning of the *Tractatus*. Moreover, what lies beyond his boundary is not a definite set of new and unfamiliar possibilities, but only a featureless void. These two aspects of the linguistic solipsism of the *Tractatus* are not easy to understand and both of them need more explanation.

The first thing that needs to be explained is the connection between classical solipsism and linguistic solipsism. The explanation is given in 5.6 and 5.61 of the *Tractatus* (quoted above, p. 96). When Wittgenstein compiled the book from entries in *Notebooks 1914–1916*, he believed that the process of logical analysis would terminate at a level where simple names could only derive their meanings directly from the objects that they designated. This restriction was a consequence of their simplicity, which was logical simplicity or indefinability. They did not have the definitions that would have allowed them to derive their meanings by a more circuitous route through the meanings of other words. They stood at the interface between language and reality, where meaning could be achieved only by direct correlation of words with things. So, of course, the things had to exist if these indefinable words were to have any meanings: in fact, the things *were* the meanings of the words at that ultimate level of analysis (see *TLP*, 3.203).

It follows that at that level any thesis about meaning will also be a thesis about existence. For Wittgenstein believed that all sentences could be analysed down to that level, and so the connection between meaning and existence would hold directly or indirectly for all sentences. Now the classical solipsist sets a limit to the things that exist, but at the interface between language and reality this becomes a limit to the sentences that make sense, and so, given that all sentences can be analysed down to this level, solipsism becomes a thesis about meaning: the sense of any sentence depends on the existence of the simple objects named in its complete analysis. This is how classical solipsism acquires its linguistic character, and this must be the basis of the insight for which Wittgenstein praises the solipsist.

It is worth noting that when Russell undertook a refutation of solipsism in his paper 'On the Nature of Acquaintance', the version that he chose for attack was the linguistic version developed in Wittgenstein's *Tractatus*.[2]

At first sight it might seem as though the experience of the present moment must be a prison for the knowledge of that moment, and as though its boundaries must be boundaries of our present world. Every word that we now understand must have a meaning that falls within our present experience; we can never point to an object and say, '*This* lies outside my present experience'. We cannot know any particular thing unless it is part of our present experience; hence it might be inferred that we cannot know that there are particular things that lie outside our present experience.     (*Monist* 1914; repr. in *Logic and Knowledge. Essays 1901–1950* (134) and now included in 'Theory of Knowledge 1913' in E. Eames and K. Blackwell (eds.), *The Collected Papers of Bertrand Russell, Vol. 7* (Allen & Unwin, 1984))

This sounds like an echo of Wittgenstein's remarks in the *Tractatus*:

The limits of my language mean the limits of my world.
   Logic pervades the world: the limits of the world are also its limits.
   So we cannot say in logic: 'The world has this in it and this, but not that.'
(*TLP*, 5.6–5.61, quoted above, p. 96 with the remainder of 5.61 and 5.62)

Or perhaps both texts originate in a discussion between the two philosophers. However, there is a great difference between Wittgenstein's development of linguistic solipsism and Russell's treatment of it. What Wittgenstein saw in it was a deep insight, but Russell argued that it is simply mistaken and set about refuting it.

Russell begins his refutation by restricting acquaintance to the present moment, and he then proceeds to argue that we can escape from imprisonment within the awareness yielded in the present moment by using inductive arguments based on the simple thought that my predictions yesterday came true today and so my predictions today will come true tomorrow.

Wittgenstein's treatment of solipsism is entirely different. He does not even think that the solipsist's claim, that the range of his knowledge is restricted to the contents of his own mind, is a factual claim. He thinks that it is something that can be shown but not said—i.e., something that is not an ordinary fact but a presupposition of thought

---

[2] *TLP*, 5.6–5.62.

and language, and, therefore not vulnerable to the kind of argument that Russell tried to use against it. This is an aspect of the general difference between the orientations of the two philosophers. When Russell wrote his Introduction to the *Tractatus* his chief point of disagreement with the book was its 'mysticism', i.e., Wittgenstein's frequent reliance on the doctrine of showing.

The difference emerges immediately in their reactions to Cartesian doubt. If I really did start my life imprisoned within the contemporary contents of my own mind, it is hard to see how I could ever escape, and Russell's attempt, like so many others, seems doomed to failure. So perhaps the starting-point is not what it seems to be. Perhaps the data from which I start are not like a map that lacks any indication of the point of origin of its grid. Maybe any attempt to read this mental map depends on some prearranged correlation between what I see on the map-sheet and objects in the world outside the map-sheet. If that were not so, the very idea of acquiring information by reading the map would collapse. It would be as if the pilot of a reconnaissance plane reported the enemy's fleet below him, but when asked for his own position, replied, 'Above the enemy's fleet'. So Wittgenstein says that the solipsist is like a person in pitch darkness who tries to give his position by saying 'I am here'.

How, then, can there be anything in solipsism? It really does look as if the correct reaction to the solipsist's claim, that only he and certain items of his mental baggage exist, is to attempt a refutation in the style of Russell. But Wittgenstein did not accept this limitation. He thought that anyone who really understood the idea that solipsism was a thesis about language would find that it opened up a new vista and a new line of inquiry.

The placing of the discussion of solipsism in the text of the *Tractatus* is enough to indicate that Wittgenstein's understanding of the doctrine is not the usual one. On its usual interpretation solipsism is vulnerable to the objection that has just been made, that it is like a map that is unreadable because it lacks a point of origin in the world outside the map-sheet. This objection would then lead naturally to a rehabilitation of the physical world in which the solipsist could find his place as an embodied observer. But Wittgenstein is going to take the linguistic character of solipsism seriously, and he signals this intention immediately by the placing of his treatment of it.

His stated aim in the *Tractatus* is to fix the boundary of meaningful discourse, and this task is completed in *TLP*, 5: all sentences that have senses are truth-functions of elementary sentences. This raises the question whether it is possible to be more specific and to set a further limit to acceptable elementary sentences; for example, perhaps we could exclude sentences containing more than a certain number of names. But he rejects all such suggestions in the 5.55s: no restrictions of this kind can be imposed on logical grounds, because 'We can foresee only what we ourselves construct' (*TLP*, 5.5563).[3]

The *application* of logic decides what elementary propositions there are.

What belongs to its application, logic cannot anticipate.

It is clear that logic must not clash with its application.

But logic has to be in contact with its application.

Therefore logic and its application must not overlap.

If I cannot say a priori what elementary propositions there are, then the attempt to do so must lead to obvious nonsense.   (*TLP*, 5.557–5.5571)

The next topic is solipsism and it is introduced in the proposition that immediately follows this one:

*The limits of my language* mean the limits of my world.   (*TLP*, 5.6)

This makes it very clear that Wittgenstein's concern is with linguistic solipsism and its implicit claim to add a further turn of the screw to the limitation of meaningful discourse. He believed that the only way to assess that claim was to achieve an understanding of the concept of the ego:

The I, the I, that is what is deeply mysterious.   (*NB*, 7-viii-16)

Russell did not share that feeling. He had simply assumed that the ego must be an object of inner sense and that the achievements of inner sense must match the achievements of outer sense. But when he tried to explain how inner sense yields knowledge of his ego, he oscillated between two different theories. In *The Problems of Philosophy* he claimed that his ego was an object of his acquaintance in spite of Hume's strong arguments against any such thesis.[4] In 'Knowledge by Acquaintance,

---

[3] This is not incompatible with the 'Vestigial Realism' of the *Tractatus*, because that is a thesis about what makes it possible to develop any 'constructions' of any kind (see above, p. 73 ff.).

[4] Russell: *The Problems of Philosophy* (Home University Library, 1912), ch. 5. See Hume's *Treatise of Human Nature*, I. iv. 6 and Appendix. In I. iv. 6 Hume claims that there is a manifest contradiction and absurdity in the suggestion that a person might have a separate internal impression of his ego, but he does not succeed in explaining

Knowledge by Description'⁵ he took the different view, that he knew his ego only by description as 'the subject term in awareness of which I am aware', but he immediately apologizes for the circularity of this definition. In 'On the Nature of Acquaintance'⁶ he suggests a way of avoiding the circularity: the description under which I know my own ego is 'the subject attending to "this", where "this" is treated as the logically proper name of a sense-datum'.

In the *Tractatus* Wittgenstein rejects both Russell's attempts to characterize my knowledge of my ego. I neither know it by acquaintance nor know it by description. In order to make these two points against Russell, he uses an idea that he derived from Schopenhauer:

The subject does not belong to the world: rather, it is a limit of the world.

Where *in* the world is a metaphysical object to be found?

You will say that this is exactly like the case of the eye and the visual field. But really you do *not* see the eye.

And nothing *in the visual field* allows you to infer that it is seen by an eye.

For the form of the visual field is surely not like this

Eye  (*TLP*, 5.632–5.6331)

This is clearly intended as a rejection of Russell's two attempts to explain knowledge of one's ego. You do not see your eye in a corner of your visual field (you are not acquainted with your ego), and nothing in your visual field supports the inference that it is seen by your eye (you do not know your ego by description).

Wittgenstein's rejection of Russell's empiricist approach to the problem of the ego hints at an alternative: we should try a neo-Kantian approach instead. For it is possible that the unity and coherence of a person's construal of the physical world is not the achievement of a single ego within his mind, but, rather, the effect of his own dual

---

what the contradiction and absurdity would be. A plausible suggestion can be derived from Wittgenstein's comparison of the field of consciousness with the visual field. My eyes do not put in an appearance in my visual field, but I can establish their function by covering them and so obliterating my visual field. But it would be sheer nonsense to suggest that I could establish the function of my ego by closing down my consciousness. For how then could I appreciate the result of this experiment?

⁵ Russell, 'Knowledge by Acquaintance, Knowledge by Description', in idem, *Mysticism and Logic* (Longmans, 1918).

⁶ Russell, 'On the Nature of Acquaintance', in idem, *Logic and Knowledge Essays, 1901–1951* (Allen & Unwin, 1951).

existence as mind and body in that world. Perhaps he himself is the hinge on which the two worlds, mental and physical, turn.

The text just quoted from the *Tractatus* (5.632–5.6331) is followed by an enigmatic comment:

This is connected with the fact that no part of our experience is at the same time a priori.

Whatever we see could be other than it is. Whatever we can describe at all could be other than it is.

There is no a priori order of things.    (*TLP*, 5.634)

The general separation of the *a priori* from the *a posteriori* (the empirical) is not controversial, and the implication of this text seems to be that, when Russell suggests that he knows his ego by description as 'the subject-term in awareness of which I am aware', he thinks mistakenly that it remains to be discovered what that subject-term is, just as when he knows his eye by description at the point of input of the visual field, it remains to be discovered which part of the surface of his body that point of input is. If this is the implication of *TLP*, 5.634, it was going to be worked out in detail in the later discussion of the geometrical eye and the physical eye in *The Blue Book*.[7]

The paradoxical character of solipsism is evident in both versions of the theory. In the traditional version, it is like a map with a grid based on a point of origin that cannot be located outside the map-sheet. In the linguistic version, this produces the further consequence that the solipsist cannot specify in detail what it is that he does not understand. Why, then, does Wittgenstein say in *TLP*, 5.62 that 'what the solipsist *means* is quite correct—only it cannot be said but makes itself manifest' (i.e. shows itself)?

It would hardly be an exaggeration to say that his thoughts about the ego in the *Tractatus* are dominated by an analogy that he derived from Schopenhauer's writings. Part of the analogy has already been discussed: a person's ego does not figure among the objects in his world, just as his eye does not put in an appearance among the things in his visual field.

It is often assumed that Wittgenstein's adoption of Schopenhauer's idea implies that he took the ego to be a myth, because the criterion of reality would be appearance in the visual field, and that is a criterion that is not satisfied by the eye. But that is a mistaken interpretation. An

---

[7]  *The Blue Book*, 63 ff., discussed below, p. 110 ff.

empiricist, like Russell, might draw that conclusion, but Wittgenstein's conclusion is different:

Thus there really is a sense in which philosophy can talk about the self in a non-psychological way.

What brings the self into philosophy is the fact that 'the world is my world'. (*TLP*, 5.641)

Russell would argue that if the ego 'came into philosophy' at all, it would have to be known either by acquaintance or by description. Wittgenstein rejected both possibilities, but nevertheless accepted the reality of the ego. Maybe he accepted its reality as a unifying function rather than as a thing, but his treatment of it in the *Tractatus* is certainly not sceptical. Nor is he sceptical about its analogue in his later philosophy, the 'geometrical eye'. He even says that I can point to my 'geometrical eye'; and so, presumably, can refer to it (*Notes for Lecture on Private Experience and Sense-data* p. 255, discussed below, p. 117 ff.).

The other part of the analogy, which is at least equally important, remains to be discussed: beyond the limit of language that a person does understand there are no failures to achieve the status of possibilities, but only a void or vacuum in which logic cannot breathe, just as there is nothing like the contents of the visual field beyond its limits.

The first feature of the analogy is easier to understand than the second one, and so it is the first feature that has received most attention from philosophers. This is because Cartesian systematic doubt seems at first to leave us with a non-problematical 'man within', a pure ego that synthesizes sensory input, and we do not worry too much about practical output. It is, of course, a mistake to concentrate on perception to the exclusion of action, and it encourages the idea that a person's mental life as a detached observer is self-sufficient. But, even if we take no account of major actions, it remains true and important that an observer still has to move around in physical space in order to acquire and synthesize the different views that he needs to get of the same object.[8] His mind needs his body and together they serve as the hinge on which the two worlds, mental and physical, turn.

Why, then, does Wittgenstein take linguistic solipsism so seriously? Why does he listen to a theory that seems to be in full flight from the physical world? One reason has already been suggested: it is a theory that, taken literally, would add a further restriction to meaningful language,

[8]  See Gareth Evans, *Varieties of Reference*, ch. 7.

but he believes that it should not be taken literally. He commends it as a dramatization of a profound truth about the limit of language. The truth is that beyond its limit there is not a whole range of candidates for the status of real possibilities waiting to be adopted and included in the list of actual senses of sentences in our language. Beyond the limit there is only a void into which we may extend our language by constructing new patterns of speech. We do this by adopting new rules of inference after they have been proved to follow from existing rules, or simply by adopting new definitions of old words. [9] We do not extend language to fit what we discover beyond its limit, because there is nothing to be discovered in a void. We can shift the limit further out into this void only by constructing extensions to existing language, and never by producing innovations to fit what we discover. There are no discoveries to be made in a void. That is the insight for which Wittgenstein commends the linguistic solipsist. [10]

What gives this insight its great importance is the fact that it is readily extendible from the solitary case—the only language that I understand—to the communal case—the only language that we understand. The common property of both languages is that beyond their limits there is not a structured manifold waiting to be described in the old ways, but only a void. Inventions are needed if we are going to succeed in extending language into this void, and though there will be constraints on the inventions, they will not be the simple constraints of applying old words in the old ways to new material acting as a cue.

This insight about the limit of language may seem remote from what the solipsist actually says:

The world is *my* world: this is manifest in the fact that the limits of *language* (of that language which alone[11] I understand) mean the limits of *my* world (*TLP*, 5.62)

However, there are several considerations which, taken together, will confirm this interpretation.

---

[9] See Ch. 2, p. 27 ff., and Ch. 4, p. 77 ff.

[10] This differs from the account of the solipsist's insight that I gave in my book *The False Prison* (Oxford, 1988). At that time, I thought that Wittgenstein commended the solipsist for realizing that all knowledge is acquired from a particular viewpoint. See *The False Prison*, i. ch. 7, But what he admired was the solipsist's *inference* from that platitude: that therefore the limit of his world can only be drawn from inside it.

[11] 'Alone' whatever else it may do, qualifies 'which'. See C. Lewy, 'A note on the text of the *Tractatus*', *Mind* (January 1967).

If someone looked at a football goal in broad daylight and said that he could only see one post, you might wonder which of the two posts his defective eyesight had shifted to make it seem to coincide with the other one. If you were not an optician, the answer might not matter, but in philosophy, when the identity of two apparently different things is asserted, it does matter which one remains attached to its usual criteria and which one has been uprooted. So when Wittgenstein expresses the solipsist's insight by saying that 'the world is my world', we want to know which of these two different things remains rooted in its old position by its usual criteria, and which one has been shifted to a position that by all its ordinary criteria is new to it.

The *Tractatus* was the first of Wittgenstein's books to be published (and the only one to be published in his lifetime), and while it stood alone it was very hard to be sure what his verdict on solipsism really meant. The question was not made any easier by the mixed ancestry of his ideas. As already explained, he was influenced by post-Kantian Idealism[12] especially by the ideas of Schopenhauer, and it seems likely that his discussions with Russell jolted him onto a parallel track, the empiricist critique of the solipsism of the Cartesian tradition. Certainly, we shall misunderstand his early treatment of the topic if we take it to be exclusively, or even primarily, concerned with solipsism based on a restriction to one's own sense-data. His primary concern was with solipsism based on the solitary ego.

It is not easy to appreciate how Wittgenstein saw the conflict between solipsism and its critics. Some light is thrown on the question by an important text in *Philosophical Remarks* (1929–1931):

That it does not strike us at all when we look around us, move about in space, feel our own bodies, etc. etc. shows how natural these things are to us. We do not notice that we see space perspectively or that our visual field is in some sense blurred towards the edges. It doesn't strike us and never can strike us because it is *the* way we perceive. We never give it a thought and it's impossible we should, since there is nothing that contrasts with the form of our world.

What I wanted to say is it's strange that those who ascribe reality only to things and not to our ideas move about so unquestioningly in the world of ideas and never long to escape from it.

In other words, how much a matter of course the given is. It would be the very devil if this were a tiny picture taken from an oblique, distorting angle.

[12] See B. McGuinness, ' "Solipsism" in the *Tractatus*', in David Charles and William Child (eds.), *Wittgensteinian Themes, Essays in honour of David Pears* (Oxford, 2001).

This, which we take as a matter of course, *life*, is supposed to be something accidental, while something that normally never comes into my head reality!

That is, what we neither can nor want to go beyond would not be the world.

Time and again the attempt is made to use language to limit the world and set it in relief—but it can't be done. The self-evidence of the world expresses itself in the very fact that language can and does only refer to it.

For since language only derives the way in which it means from its meaning, from the world, no language is conceivable that does not represent this world. (*Philosophical Remarks*, S v 47)

In the *Tractatus* the point had been made more concisely: 'The world and life are one' (*TLP*, 5.621).

It is, therefore impossible to drive a wedge between our general conception of the world and the way things really are in the world and it is a mistake to call the realism of daily life 'naïve'. This is the leading idea of Wittgenstein's later philosophy and it is based on something more than our passive reception of information about the world. We are also agents who intervene in the course of nature and the results of our interventions provide criteria of the way things are in the world. Reality is life.

These ideas dominate Wittgenstein's later philosophy, but they are already developing in his early treatment of solipsism.[13] As usual, this is easier to see in the more experimental discussions in the *Notebooks* than in the final version published in the *Tractatus*. In the *Notebooks* he presents his investigation of solipsism as a journey which returns him to its starting-point, but returns him with a better understanding of what the nature of that starting-point really was.

This is the way I have travelled: Idealism singles men out from the world as unique, solipsism singles me alone out, and at last I see that I too belong with the rest of the world, and so on the one side *nothing* is left over, and on the other side there remains something really unique, *the world*. Thus idealism leads to realism if it is strictly thought out.[14]    (*NB* 15-x-16)

The stages of this journey are different philosophical theories, each of which, as he says in *PR* S 47, tries to use language to limit the world and

---

[13] See Derek Bolton, 'Life-form and Idealism', in G. Vesey (ed.), *Idealism, Past and Present* (Cambridge, 1982), 269–82.

[14] The translation has been slightly altered. It is worth noting that the description of this journey in the *Tractatus* is different: 'Here it can be seen that solipsism, when its implications are followed out strictly, coincides with pure realism. The self of solipsism shrinks to a point without extension and there remains the reality co-ordinated with it.' (*TLP*, 5.64).

set it in relief. But it can't be done. Solipsism attempts this impossible task by giving the theorist's ego the pivotal role. The corrective is to see that

The human body, however, my body in particular, is a part of the world among others, among animals, plants, stones etc. etc.

Whoever realizes this will not want to procure a preferential place for his own body or for the human body.

He will regard humans and animals quite naively as objects which are similar and belong together.   (*NB* 2-ix-16)

So, though he mentions with approval, or at least with appreciation, the idea that there is a single spirit common to all sentient beings (*NB* 15.x.16), he maintains that it can only function in its separate embodiments in individual sentient beings.

But what happened in his later work to the insight for which he commended the solipsist? Apparently two transformations occurred. First, the solitary case, myself, was replaced by the community, ourselves, the speakers of a common language. Second, the project of drawing a single boundary around the whole of factual language was abandoned and the heir to that project was a piecemeal investigation of the bounds of sense reinforced by a therapeutic treatment of different attempts to trespass beyond them.

My aim is to teach you to pass from a piece of disguised nonsense to something that is patent nonsense.   (*PI* I, S 464)

So the boundary between sense and nonsense is no longer a continuous line drawn by the application of a single theory of meaning, but more like a series of road-blocks placed on individual deviations from sense into nonsense. When this piecemeal approach had replaced the geometric theory of the *Tractatus*, the solipsist's insight did not have to be abandoned but only reformulated to fit the complexity of the new situation. It remained true that beyond each road-block there was only a vacuum and not a candidate hoping for recognition as a real possibility.[15]

The other aspect of Wittgenstein's treatment of solipsism in the *Tractatus* was his account of the ego, and the sequel to his early ideas on that topic is less difficult to identify. It consists in a highly imaginative development of the short text in the *Tractatus* in which he had adopted

---

[15] So in his discussion of the source of the incompatibility of two complementary colours, he asks, 'But what is the right simile here? That of a road that is physically impassable, or of the non-existence of a road?' (Zettel, S 356–8, quoted above, p. 80).

Schopenhauer's comparison of the relation of the ego to the contents of the mind with the relation of the eye to the contents of the visual field (*TLP*, 5.632–5.6331, quoted and discussed above, p. 103).

This development occurs in *The Blue Book* in a passage where Wittgenstein draws two parallel distinctions. One is the distinction between the treatment of the ego as an abstract, elusive subject that cannot be pinned down to anything empirically identifiable and the treatment of people in daily life, where they figure in a perfectly ordinary way as bodies with minds. He then illustrates the nature of this distinction by drawing another, parallel distinction between the eye identified as the physical organ of sight and what he calls 'the geometrical eye'. The physical eye is, of course, identified as a particular part of the body, but the geometrical eye is the focal point behind the reception of optical stimulation, an abstract entity without an independent criterion of identity. These two distinctions are developed on parallel lines, and the abstract character of the geometrical eye is used to illustrate the abstract character of the elusive ego. This is evidently a development of *Tractatus* 5.632–5.633

In *the Blue Book* he imagines that he makes a solipsistic statement in these words: 'When anything is seen, it is always I who see', and he asks 'What is it I want all these cases of seeing to have in common?' He says: 'As an answer I have to confess to myself that it is not my bodily appearance. I don't always see part of my body when I see. And it isn't essential that my body, if seen among the things that I see, should always look the same. In fact, I don't mind how much it changes. And I feel the same way about all the properties of my body, the characteristics of my behaviour, and even about my memories.—When I think about it a little longer I see that what I wished to say was, "Always when anything is seen, something is seen." I.e. that of which I said it continued during all the experiences of seeing was not any particular "I", but the experience of seeing itself. This may become clearer if we imagine the man who makes our solipsistic statement to point to his eyes when he says "I". (Perhaps because he wishes to be exact and wants to say expressly which eyes belong to the mouth that says "I" and to the hands pointing to his own body.) But what is he pointing to? These particular eyes with the identity of physical objects? (To understand this sentence, you must remember that the grammar of words of which we say that they stand for physical objects is characterized by the way in which we use the phrase "the *same* so and so" or "the identical so and so", where "so and so" designates the physical object.) We said before that he did not wish to point to a particular physical object at all. The idea that he had made a significant statement arose from a confusion corresponding to the confusion between what we shall call "The geometrical eye" and "the physical eye" '. (*The Blue Book*, 63)

There is, of course, no doubt about the criteria of pointing to his physical eye(s). He can rely on his knowledge of the part of the surface of his body that is discriminatingly sensitive to light-rays. Or, to make the demonstration more convincing, he can watch what he does in a mirror while he is doing it. The criteria of pointing to his 'geometrical eye' are quite different: he will bring his index finger in on the central axis of the space that he sees in front of him until it reaches its maximum size and then is seen no more.[16] When he does this he might end up pointing to his navel or even to empty space above his head, but, fortunately, that never happens.

This is a development of the treatment of the ego in the *Tractatus*: you do not see the eye that does the seeing, and similarly you are not conscious of the ego that is the subject of consciousness.[17] But *The Blue Book* text takes the discussion much further. It begins, like the *Tractatus* text, as a critique of solipsism, but it soon develops into a general investigation of the relation between the world of experience and the physical world.

One conclusion that might be drawn from this investigation is that the kind of experiment that would identify the eye as the point of input of visual data cannot be duplicated within the mind, because there is no parallel way of identifying the ego as the ultimate point of their reception. This would have provided Hume with an argument stronger than his mere assertion that, as a matter of fact, he does not have an inner impression of his self (see above, pp. 102–103, n. 4).

But the two lessons that Wittgenstein seems to draw from this investigation are more far-reaching. One is that it casts doubt on the suggestion that the pronoun 'I' functions as a referential expression. The other is that it throws light on his treatment of Private Language. Both these connections of thought involve difficult questions of interpretation.

---

[16] This is somewhat like the auditory system once used by aeroplanes landing in poor visibility. The pilot flies in to the point of a cone with its boundaries marked for him by a bell ringing if he deviates outside the cone. A similar olfactory system is used by the males of some species of flying insects when they are seeking the females. A cone of scent downwind of the females guides the males to them. See J.-H. Fabre, 'The Great Peacock Moth', in *Social Life in the Insect World*. The flight of males using this method looks very haphazard because it oscillates between the two sides of the cone in a way that does not look purposive, and in the 18th century lepidopterists called one species that used this method 'The Vapourer'.

[17] *TLP*, 5.633–5.6331, quoted above, p. 103.

Consider, first, the connection between his critique of solipsism and his critique of Private Language. He treats both theories as attempts to skim a slice from the one and only world, and to set it up as another, independent, world. In *Philosophical Remarks* (S 47, quoted above, pp. 107–108), when he rejects the attempt to set up an independent world of sensory experiences, he does not explicitly make the connection with solipsism, but in S 48 he does equate 'the stream of life' with 'the stream of the world' in words that echo some enigmatic remarks about solipsism in the *Tractatus*:

5.621 The world and life are one.

5.63 I am my world. (The microcosm.)

5.631 There is no such thing as the subject that thinks or entertains ideas.

> If I wrote a book called *The World as I found it*, I should have to include a report on my body, and should have to say which parts were subordinate to my will, and which were not, etc., this being a method of isolating the subject, or rather of showing that in an important sense there is no subject; for it alone could *not* be mentioned in that book. (*TLP* 5.621–5.631)

Later, in a passage in *Notes for Lectures* in which he is developing his critique of Private Language, he considers the common objection that his account leaves something out:

> It seems that I neglect life. But not life physiologically understood but life as consciousness. And consciousness not physiologically understood, or understood from the outside, but consciousness as the very essence of experience, the appearance of the world, the world. ('Notes for Lectures', in Klagge and Nordmann (eds.), *Ludwig Wittgenstein: Philosophical Occasions, 1912–1951*, 255)

Here we have the same equation of ideas: sensory experience in its place in the world is life. In fact, in his later philosophy it is axiomatic that our inner and outer lives are inseparable. The text quoted above ((pp. 000–00), *Philosophical Remarks*, S 47) leaves no doubt about this and it is the justification of the new philosophical method that he began to follow in 1929. S 47 ends with a conclusion that is worth repeating:

> Time and again the attempt is made to use language to limit the world and set it in relief—but it can't be done. The self-evidence of the world expresses itself in the very fact that language can and does only refer to it.
> For since language only derives the way in which it means from its meaning, from the world, no language is conceivable which does not represent the world. (PR S 47)

The discussion in *Notes for Lectures* is especially interesting because in it the connection between his critique of Solipsism and his critique of Private Language is not left to our conjecture, but is explicit:

> 'But aren't you neglecting something—the experience or whatever you might call it—? Almost *the world* behind the mere words?' [The critic is speaking]
>
> But here solipsism teaches us a lesson: It is that thought which is *on the way* to destroy this idea. For if the *world* is idea, it isn't any person's idea. (Solipsism stops short of saying this and says that it is my idea.) But then how could I say what the world is if the realm of ideas has no neighbour? What I do comes to defining the word 'world'.
>
> 'I neglect that which goes without saying.'
>
> 'What is seen *I* see' (pointing to my body). I point at my geometrical eye, saying this.[18] Or I point with closed eyes and touch my breast and feel it. In no case do I make a connection between what is seen and a person. ('Notes for Lectures on "Private Experience" and "Sense-Data" in Klagge and Nordmann (eds.), *Ludwig Wittgenstein: Philosophical Occasions, 1912–1951*, 255')

It is easier to see that this tantalizing text is important than it is to explain its importance. First, we need to understand the remark about the geometrical eye. The words 'What is seen *I* see' are intended as an expression of solipsism. For they are almost identical with the words used by the solipsist in *The Blue Book*: 'When anything is seen it is always I who see' (*BB*, 63), quoted above, pp. 110–111]. That is why Wittgenstein says that, when I point to my body in the way in which a solipsist points to his body, I am not really pointing to myself as an embodied person but only pointing to my geometrical eye, the pure ego, which is not attached to any person—not even to myself—but is a free-floating subjectivity.[19]

But what exactly is the lesson that solipsism teaches us? In this passage he is developing his critique of Private Language and so the lesson must contribute something to that critique. Now the conclusion of the

---

[18] i.e., I point *through* my body *at* my geometrical eye. That is why he goes on to say that I do not make a connection between what is seen and a person with a body as well as a mind.

[19] I am tempted to say, 'It seems at least a fact of experience that at the source of *the visual field* there is mostly a small man with grey flannel trousers, in fact L.W.' —Someone might answer this to me: It is true that you almost always wear grey flannel trousers and often look at them.

'But I am in a favoured position. I am the centre of the world.' Suppose I saw myself in the mirror saying this, and pointing to myself, would it still be all right?

When I say I play a unique role, I really mean the geometrical eye. (*Ludwig Wittgenstein: Philosophical Occasions 1912–1951*, ed. Klagge and Nordmann, 257).

critique is going to be that any attempt to detach the world of human experience (in Schopenhauer's terminology 'the world as idea') from the physical world will always be a mistake. But how does solipsism teach us to avoid this mistake? Surely solipsism is only a very extreme example of the general mistake and not a way of avoiding it?

But though that is true, it is not the whole truth of the matter. If we look back at the treatment of solipsism in the *Tractatus*, we can see that he regarded it not just as a theory—'Take it or leave it'—but as a necessary stage of an intellectual journey from confusion to enlightenment. The error made by the solipsist is an example of the general error of detaching the world of experience from the physical world and the theory of Private Language is another example of the same error. In the case of Private Language the mistaken assumption is that, when someone reports a sensation, there is something inaccessible to public language sandwiched between the stimulus and his response to it. In the case of solipsism the mistake is the assumption that behind any set of experiences there is an inaccessible focal point, a pure ego. But solipsism is also *on the way* to destroying this error, because it is the theory of a philosopher who is on the move. He feels obliged to retreat to his solipsistic position, but then finds that he cannot rest there but must move on to the next stage, which is a flat perceptual Realism.

This cycle of delusion and enlightenment is described in the *Tractatus* but more fully and explicitly in the *Notebooks*: 'This is the way I have travelled ...' (*NB*, 15-x-1916). However, the early version in the *Notebooks* makes the journey start from Idealism, while the later version in the *Tractatus* makes it start from solipsism (see above, p. 96). The early version gives a more complete picture of the movement of thought and so a better explanation of Wittgenstein's remark that solipsism is *on the way* to destroying the error. This, of course, is the point from which his therapeutic conception of philosophy developed.

The driving force behind the movement from one theory to the next is, in this case, scepticism about the physical world, which is then followed by scepticism about the meaning of any theory that tries to dispense with the physical world. What could such a theory mean by 'The world'? (cf. *PR* S 47, quoted above, pp. 107–108).

The remaining remarks on this page of the *Notes for Lectures* give more details of the connection between his treatment of solipsism in the *Tractatus* and his treatment of Private Language in his later writings. First, he makes the point that, since language can only be about the one and only world, there is no need for a special word to be added to every proposition in order to draw attention to what is a natural limitation.

> Couldn't I say: If I had to add the world to my language it would have to be one sign for the whole of language, which sign could therefore be left out. ('Notes for Lectures', Klagge and Nordmann: *Ludwig Wittgenstein: Philosophical Occasions 1912–1951*, 255)

This, too, should be compared with *Philosophical Remarks*, S 47. Then finally he returns to the charge that in his critique of *Private Language* he leaves out the very thing that makes the difference between a true report of a sensation and a false one.

> 'But it seems as if you were neglecting something.' But what more can I do than *distinguish* the case of saying 'I have toothache' when I really have toothache, and the case of saying the words without having toothache. I am also (further) ready to talk of any x behind the words so long as it keeps its identity.
>
> Isn't what you reproach me of [*sic*] as though you said 'In your language you are only *speaking*'? (Ibid., 256)

His defence is that he is including in his account everything that has a genuine criterion of identity. If the sensation were removed from its position between stimulus and response, it would be left without a criterion of identity. This is the essence of his critique of Private Language. That is one lesson that solipsism teaches us.


## THE SECOND PARADOX

The other lesson that Wittgenstein seems to extract from the development of his early treatment of solipsism is that the pronoun 'I' is not a referential expression. This is highly paradoxical for a reason that has already been explained: if a person's name is used to refer to him, surely the personal pronoun 'I', which he alone can use to replace his name, will also be used to refer to him (see above, p. 97). It is paradoxical to deny this and, unlike the paradox of crediting the solipsist with a good point, this one does not depend on any exclusively philosophical theory. It only requires a knowledge of grammar.

What makes this paradox especially hard to accept is its context. Wittgenstein formulated it after 1929, when his philosophy veered in a new direction and what Elizabeth Anscombe once called 'the big music of the *Tractatus*' was only rarely heard. Grand theories no longer played the role of Homeric gods, intervening directly in human affairs, but made themselves felt from behind the scenes of ordinary life, which now became his concern.

> ... we may not advance any kind of theory. There must not be anything hypothetical in our considerations. We must do away with all *explanation* and description alone must take its place. And this description gets its light, that is to say its purpose, from the philosophical problems. These are, of course, not empirical problems; they are solved, rather by looking into the workings of our language, and that in such a way as to make us recognize those workings *in despite of* an urge to misunderstand them. The problems are solved not by giving new information, but by arranging what we have always known. Philosophy is a battle against the bewitchment of our intelligence by means of language.    (*PI* I, S 109, quoted above, pp. 0 and p. 00)

After this manifesto, which introduces his new way of dealing with philosophical problems, it is extremely surprising to find him denying that the word 'I' makes a reference. An examination of the use of 'I' in daily life would never support that verdict.

However, it is indisputable that it is the verdict that he reached. His unequivocal formulation of his conclusion, quoted above, (pp. 110–111) from *The Blue Book* is worth repeating:

> To say 'I have pain' is no more a statement *about* a particular person than moaning is. But surely the word 'I' in the mouth of a man refers to the man who says it: it points to himself, and very often a man who says it actually points to himself with his finger. But it was quite superfluous to point to himself. He might just as well only have raised his hand.    (*The Blue Book* (1933–1934), 66–7)

This is endorsed two years later in *Notes for Lecture on Private Experience and Sense-data*. 'The word "I" does not designate a person (bezeichnet keine Person)' (*Ludwig Wittgenstein: Philosophical Occasions 1912–1951*, ed. Klagge and Nordmann, 228). The point is repeated in MS 116, p. 215.

But what reason can he have had for this paradoxical denial? Was he harking back to the doctrine of the *Tractatus*, that the ego is not an object of any kind and, therefore, not a possible target of reference, but, rather, 'a limit of the world' (*TLP*, 5.632)? But that line of thought had not led him to deny that the word 'I' is referential, but only to formulate a more carefully qualified conclusion,

> Thus there really is a sense in which philosophy can talk about the self in a non-psychological way.

What brings the self into philosophy is the fact that 'the world is my world'. (*TLP*, 5. 641)

This neo-Kantian reformulation of the status of the ego, based on the paradoxical assessment of solipsism, seems to leave without an answer the question that needs to be answered before we can understand the second paradox. 'If the ego is not presented to inner sense in one of the two ways suggested by Russell, does it follow that it cannot be a target of reference?' To put the question in the terminology of *The Blue Book*, is it impossible for me to refer to my 'geometrical eye'?[20]

Before we go any further, it is worth asking why these questions are so difficult to answer. The reason is that there is a geological fault between Wittgenstein's pre-1918 philosophy and his post-1929 philosophy, and it is very difficult to be sure of continuities running across the fault-line. When he was doing the preliminary work for the *Tractatus* the problems were set by the theories of other philosophers, but after 1929 they were set by plain facts about ordinary thought and language. It is always difficult to trace the development of his ideas against these two disparate backgrounds and nowhere more difficult than in his philosophy of persons.

So we must not expect an easy answer to the question how Wittgenstein's later denial of the referentiality of 'I' is related to his earlier doctrine, that the ego is not an object of any kind and, therefore, not a possible target of reference. It is not even clear that a person cannot refer to his 'geometrical eye'. There is a passage in *Notes for Lectures* which implies that it is a possible target of reference:

What is seen *I* see (pointing at my body). I point at my geometrical eye, saying this. Or I point with closed eyes and touch my breast and feel it. In no case do I make a connection between what is seen and a person. (*Notes for Lectures*, 255)

So it seems that I can point through my body at the focal point where optical stimulation is received.[21] This, of course, is a new species of reference: I do not see that my shot hits its target and so I can only have indirect evidence of its success (see below, pp. 124–125).

But the most important difference between Wittgenstein's later examination of the pronoun 'I' and his earlier examination of it is his almost exclusive concentration on its use in communication between two or more people, and his comparative neglect of the problem of the elusive ego. Whatever happened to the problem of the ego, it was not

[20] See above, pp. 110–111.    [21] See above, p. 113, n. 18.

going to help to explain how I convey to another person the identity of the person about whom I am speaking. That is achieved by the use of the pronouns 'you', 'he', 'I', etc., and the question is 'how do they work'?

In *Notes for Lectures* Wittgenstein gives the most important part of the answer:

Remember that, whatever the word 'I' means to you, to the other man it shows/draws his attention to/a human body and is of no value otherwise.[22]

This remark reveals the distance between the problem of the elusive ego and the problem of the referentiality of 'I'. If 'I' does refer, the target of its reference will now be the physical aspect of a psycho-physical entity and not something purely psychical. That opens up a gulf between the early discussions of the ego and the later discussions of the ways in which people communicate with one another about themselves and about others. If Wittgenstein now concludes that 'I' is non-referential, that will have to be for a reason that is entirely different from his earlier denial of its referentiality. For the elusiveness of the ego will now be irrelevant to the task that confronts two people who are talking to each other about one another. Their task is to indicate about whom their remarks are intended to be and they can use their bodies to help them carry out this task. So why, in this new context, does he deny that 'I' makes a reference? The denial is deeply mysterious.

It does not seem possible to connect this denial in any straightforward way with the doctrines of the *Tractatus*. However, it might, perhaps, be construed as a natural development of some other line of thought that started after 1929. Now there are, in fact, two texts written soon after 1929 that might help to explain his paradoxical denial that 'I' makes a reference. Both start new lines of thought that are not to be found in the *Tractatus* even in an embryonic form. One is the much-discussed text in which he distinguishes two uses of 'I'—its use as subject and its use as object (*Blue Book*, 66–7). The other text proposes a way of eliminating the word 'I' altogether from my reports of my own sensations (*Philosophical Remarks* SS 58–64).

Here is *The Blue Book* text:

Now the idea that the real I lives in my body is connected with the peculiar grammar of the word 'I', and the misunderstanding this grammar is liable

---

[22] *Ludwig Wittgenstein: Philosophical Occasions 1912–1951*, ed. J. Klagge and A. Nordmann, 228. This reminder occurs in a passage where he flatly denies that 'I' designates a person. What he is asserting is only that there must be some connection between the speaker's use of 'I' and his body, even if the connection is not designation or reference.

to give rise to. There are two different cases in the use of the word 'I' (or 'my') which I might call 'the use as object' and 'the use as subject'. Examples of the first kind of use are these: 'My arm is broken', 'I have grown six inches', 'I have a bump on my forehead', 'The wind blows my hair about'. Examples of the second kind are '*I* see so-and-so', '*I* hear so-and-so', '*I* try to lift my arm', '*I* think it will rain', '*I* have toothache'. One can point to the difference between these two categories by saying: the cases of the first category involve the recognition of a particular person, and there is in these cases the possibility of an error, or, as I should rather put it: the possibility of an error has been provided for. The possibility of failing to score has been provided for in a pin game. On the other hand, it is not one of the hazards of the game that the balls should fail to come up if I have put a penny in the slot. It is possible that, say in an accident, I should feel a pain in my arm, see a broken arm at my side, and think it is mine, when really it is my neighbour's. And I could, looking into a mirror, mistake a bump on his forehead for one on mine. On the other hand, there is no question of recognizing a person when I say I have toothache. To ask 'Are you sure that its *you* who have pains?' would be nonsensical. Now, when in this case no error is possible, it is because the move which we might be inclined to think of as an error, a 'bad move', is no move in the game at all. . . . And now this way of stating our idea suggests itself: that it is as impossible that in making the statement 'I have toothache' I should have mistaken another person for myself, as it is to moan with pain by mistake, having mistaken someone else for me. To say 'I have pain' is no more a statement *about* a particular person than moaning is. But surely the word 'I' in the mouth of a man refers to the man who says it; it points to himself, and very often a man who says it actually points to himself with his finger. But it was quite superfluous to point to himself. He might just as well only have raised his hand.    (*The Blue Book*, 66–7)

This famous text[23] is rich in detail and the first question that needs to be asked about it is 'what do the uses of "I" as subject have in common?' Evidently the answer is that the information—for example, the information that I have toothache—is delivered on the inner circuit of my nervous system when I feel the toothache.[24] There is, therefore, a sharp contrast with 'the use of "I" as object', where the information is delivered on a track passing through a point that is equally accessible to other people. For example, suppose that I base the statement 'I have a bump on my forehead' on the fact that I see in a mirror a reflection of a man with

---

[23] Discussed in detail in G. Evans, *Varieties of Reference* (Oxford, 1981), ch. 7 and Appendix.
[24] If I feel it, it must be mine. That is guaranteed by the integrity and isolation of my nervous system.

a bump on his forehead and I take him to be myself. In that case, the information is delivered on a track that passes through the physical world outside my nervous system and is, therefore, accessible to other people. When the information comes to me in this way, on a public track, I can be mistaken—the man reflected in the mirror might be someone else.[25]

The second text which starts a new line of thought after 1929 and might help to explain why Wittgenstein denies the referentiality of 'I', occurs in *Philosophical Remarks* (1929–1931).[26] Wittgenstein suggests that it would be possible to use a language that lacked the word 'I'. Instead of saying that someone else was in pain I would say that he was behaving as I did when I was in pain; and when I was in pain, I would simply say 'There is pain.' The first-person case would be the default case with no explicit identification of the sufferer, who would then be understood to be the speaker.[27]

A little later in *Philosophical Remarks* he comments on the way in which we actually do report our pains. We say 'I have a pain.' But

'I have a pain' is a sign of a completely different kind when I am using the proposition from what it is to me on the lips of another; the reason being that it is senseless, as far as I'm concerned, on the lips of another, until I know through which mouth it was expressed. The propositional sign in this case doesn't consist in the sound alone, but in the fact that the sound came out of this mouth. Whereas in the case in which I say or think it, the sign is the sound itself.   (Ibid., S 64)

It is not immediately clear what point he is making in this text. It is, of course, obvious that, if I hear the words 'I am in pain', I shall not get

---

[25]  This is what Harpo Marx suspected might be the case in the famous mirror scene in the film *Duck Soup*. But the use of 'I' as object does not have to involve a mirror. I could point to myself in a group photograph and say, 'You see, I was slimmer in those days.' It does not even need a visual cue. I could read a report of an act of heroism in battle and I could say, 'You see, I deserved my medal.' (See my article, 'Saying and Doing: The Pragmatic Aspect of Wittgenstein's Treatment of "I"', in Weingartner, Schurz and Dorn, Holder, Pichter, Tempsky (eds.), *The Role of Pragmatics in Contemporary Philosophy*, (Vienna, 1999).

Wittgenstein's example, the broken arm which is not mine is a little implausible. But Tolstoy describes Prince Andrei's death in battle as an event that he witnesses, with his own eyes but as if it were happening to someone else. Cf. W. James's anecdote about the man Baldy, who fell out of a carriage and commented 'Poor Baldy!' as if he were only a witness of someone else's accident (cited by Elizabeth Anscombe in her article 'The First Person', in S. Guttenplan (ed.), *Mind and Language* (Oxford, 1975), 45–65).

[26]  Ludwig Wittgenstein, *Philosophical Remarks* (Basil Blackwell, 1975), S 58.

[27]  This is sometimes called 'the no-ownership theory' of things in the mind, but its point is that there is no separate owner and no separate representation of any owner.

the message until I find out who uttered them, but will only believe that *someone* is in pain. That is the point that is usually made by calling the word 'I' a 'token-reflexive' expression. But Wittgenstein makes it in a different way: he says that when I hear someone else uttering the words, his mouth will be part of the propositional sign, but when I myself utter them, the propositional sign consists in the words alone. In *The Blue Book* he says that 'The man who cries out with pain, or says that he has pain does not choose the mouth which says it.'[28] He could have added that nobody can ever choose the mouth through which he produces any utterance. Even a ventriloquist can only make his vocalizations *seem* to come out of another person's mouth. That they might *really* come out of another person's mouth is not a possibility for creatures whose nervous systems are isolated from one another as ours are. So Wittgenstein says that his mouth is not part of the propositional sign when he himself utters the words: he could have said that it is part of the propositional sign, but a part which he cannot avoid using.

In *Notes for Lectures* he offers what seems to be a different explanation of his claim that 'I don't choose the mouth which says "I have toothache."' 'If I say "*I* see this" I am liable to tap my chest to show which person I am. Now suppose I had no head and pointing to my geometrical eye I would point to an empty space above my neck, wouldn't I still feel that I pointed to the person who sees, tapping my chest?'[29] Now I might ask 'How do I know in this case who sees this?' But what is *this*? It's no use just pointing ahead of me, and if, instead, I point to a description and tap both my chest and the description and say '*I see this*'—it has no sense to ask 'How do you know that its *you* who see it? For I don't *know* that it's this person and not another one which sees before I point, but one could, in certain cases, say I know *because* I point.—This is what I meant by saying that I don't choose the mouth which says "I have toothache."'[30]

This is obscure, like much of the rapid thinking in Wittgenstein's notes. He is developing an alternative to the Cartesian account of the way in which a person is related to things within his own mind. According to that account he—or rather an inner representative such as his ego—notices the occurrence of an impression—for example,

---

[28] This point is repeated in *The Blue Book*, p. 68.
[29] This bizarre possibility is explained above, p. 111.
[30] 'Notes for Lectures' in *Ludwig Wittgenstein: Philosophical Occasions 1912–1951*, ed. J. Klagge and A. Nordmann, 274.

a visual impression of something in the physical world—points to it and refers to it. This story is modelled on the pattern of pointing and reference in an ordinary situation in the physical world: for example, a sergeant-major, confronted by a line of soldiers points at one of them and shouts 'You! Yes, I mean you.' Now this analogy requires us to be able to give a convincing account of the 'man within' or ego. It also needs a convincing account of the group from which a single individual is selected as the target of reference. Wittgenstein's general strategy is to argue that no such accounts can be given.

The flaws in the story of the ego have already been discussed. This difficult text moves on to a discussion of the flaws in the account of what it is supposed to do. Wittgenstein argues that, if there were such an ego, its mode of operation would be unlike the sergeant-major's. He knows which soldier he wants to reprimand, points to him and refers to him, but this three-step procedure would not be matched by anything that an ego might do in a person's mind. For the sergeant-major points to the delinquent soldier because he knows who he is, but the situation of the ego, if an ego were involved, would be the reverse—it would know because it pointed. At least, that is what Wittgenstein appears to be saying in this difficult text.

An example may help to make his idea clearer. So suppose that I am stung by a wasp and immediately clap my hand to the source of the pain. I know that it is I who have been hurt at that point, because that is guaranteed by the isolation of my nervous system.[31] including this particular reflex arc. So when I say, 'The wasp has got me', that will be a perfect example of the use of 'I' ('me') as subject. There is no point in the drama at which someone else could have insinuated himself and taken my place in it. 'I know *because* I point' unlike the sergeant-major, who points because he knows.

This is an advance beyond the theory of the ego which operates within the mind in much the same way as the complete person operates in the physical world. The ego would not always have to select a target of reference from an array of possible targets within the mind, like the sergeant-major with the soldiers. Sometimes the connection would be made for it automatically and without the person's having any knowledge of the target beyond the knowledge that the required

---

[31] Wittgenstein was not a physicalist and so he would say that my claim to knowledge is guaranteed by the isolation of my mind, including all its reflex arcs, and the isolation of my mind is guaranteed by the isolation of my nervous system.

connection with it had been made. In such a case the line of reference retraces the epistemic line which connects him with its target, but retraces it in the reverse direction.[32]

This is an improvement on the theory of the ego operating in the mind in the same way that the complete person operates in the physical world. It allows for the possibility of making a definite reference without consciously identifying its target before making it. This type of reference would be like indirect artillery fire, where the man on the gun does not see the target, but takes instructions from someone else who does see it.

However, it leaves many questions about the development of Wittgenstein's philosophy of mind unanswered. For example, why does he end the passage quoted from *Notes for Lectures* by saying, 'This is what I meant by saying that I don't choose the mouth which says "I have toothache" '?[33] Surely, *whatever* I say, I don't choose the mouth that says it. So the lack of choice has no special connection with the extension to his theory of reference that preceded it. The peculiarity of this case is that what I do not choose is, paradoxically, part of the proposition.[34]

What makes this extension of the theory of reference important is that it removes the Cartesian need to assume that reference within the mind must operate in exactly the same way as reference in the physical world. So when we find that reference within the mind does not have to involve conscious selection from a group of possible targets, we do not have to conclude that it cannot really be reference, and we are free to explore the possibility that it might be reference with a different structure.

The structure suggested by Wittgenstein in the enigmatic text quoted above from *Notes for Lectures* (*Notes for Lectures*, 274)) seems to be a development of his early Kantian ideas about the ego. In *The Blue Book* he tells us what was wrong with those ideas: they encourage the mistake of confusing the 'geometrical eye' with the person (see above, pp. 110–111). But there might, nevertheless, be some truth in them, and that truth might be inherited by the enigmatic account of reference within the mind that has just been analysed.

This is only a conjecture, but perhaps it merits a sketch of the way in which it might be developed. Kant's transcendental unity of

[32] See my article, 'Saying and Doing: The Pragmatic Aspect of Wittgenstein's Treatment of "I"'.

[33] *Notes for Lectures*, 274, quoted above, p. 121.

[34] See above, p. 120.

apperception was meant to be a function rather than a thing. Its effect was to produce connections between ideas based on their subjective ownership. But perhaps the connections could be explained as the product of the dynamics of individual nervous systems. 'I know because I point.'

The difference between the structure of this kind of case and the structure of an ordinary case of reference to something in the physical world is easily missed and worth emphasizing. Someone who refers to an object in the physical world begins by picking it out from its background and then uses its distinguishing marks to point it out to his audience. This encourages the idea that all cases of reference must have this structure, and so we overlook the cases where automatic pointing comes first and the distinguishing mark of the target is just that it has been the target of automatic pointing. This is a case of reason mistrusting its own origins. A respectable reference is one that can be supported by a list of the distinguishing marks of its target, but why should we be impressed by a reference whose only support is the fact that its target is a natural target of automatic pointing? This is like a question about the validity of descriptions that was raised in Chapter 2: why should we trust descriptions that are applied to things at the interface between language and the world, where the only reason that we can give for applying them is that we find them natural.[35] But what better reason could there be?

Whatever the answer to that question, Wittgenstein leaves us in no doubt about the importance of the difference between reference supported by independent distinguishing marks and basic automatic pointing.

The mouth which says 'I' or the hand which is raised to indicate that it is I who wish to speak, or I who have toothache, does not thereby point to anything. If, on the other hand, I wish to indicate the *place* of my pain, I point. And here again remember the difference between pointing to the painful spot without being led by the eye and on the other hand pointing to a scar on my body after looking for it. ('That's where I was vaccinated.')—The man who cries out with pain, or says that he has pain, *doesn't choose the mouth which says it.*    (*The Blue Book*, 68)

In this passage the example of the new type of reference is 'pointing to the painful spot without being led by the eye.' This is like the example

---

[35] See above, p. 19.

used above, clapping my hand to the place where I have been stung by a wasp (see above, p. 122). In such cases reference is not guided by a prior specification of its target and, before I point, all that I know about the target is that it is what my pointing will indicate. The accuracy of the indication, when it does occur, is guaranteed not by my previous knowledge, as it would be guaranteed in a typical case of reference, but by the compulsive force of the automatic operation of a reflex arc.

This passage in *The Blue Book* is also interesting for another reason: it continues by developing an argument for his paradoxical refusal to allow that 'I' is a referential expression.

He had already given an argument of a sort for this denial in a passage quoted earlier from *The Blue Book*:

But it was quite superfluous to point to himself. He might just as well only have raised his hand. (*The Blue Book*, 67, quoted above, p. 119)

However, that is not a strong argument: it merely reminds us that there are alternatives to pointing to one's self available to a speaker who uses the word 'I'; and so, if pointing to one's self is the typical accompaniment of self-reference, in cases where it does not occur some doubt is cast on the referential character of 'I', but not much doubt.

But there is what may be a stronger argument for his denial of its referential character in the sequel to the passage quoted above from p. 68 of *The Blue Book*. Unfortunately it is difficult to identify the structure of this argument. It appears to be based on Wittgenstein's view of 'the difference between the propositions "I have pain" and "He has pain"'. Now we might expect him to say that it is simply 'the difference between "L.W. has pain" and "Smith" [if that is his name] "has pain"'. But he does not say that. What he says instead is this: 'Rather, it corresponds to the difference between moaning and saying that someone moans.'[36] On the next page he comments, 'When we feel that we wish to abolish the I in "I have pain", one may say that we tend to make the verbal expression of pain similar to the expression by moaning' (Ibid., 69).

What is going on here? We might protest that the question about the function of 'I' is a general one, and so it is inappropriate to try to answer it by focusing onto a single kind of first-person report, 'I have pain' narrowly interpreted as expressive.

---

[36] This ignores a possibility that he never denied and later allowed to be important: a person in pain might coolly state that fact. e.g. when he was being examined by a doctor. It is also important that exteroceptive sensations often lack a single natural expression. See Ch. 3.

But what *is* going on in this strange discussion of the difference between 'I have pain' and 'He has pain'? The clue to answering this question is given in the discussion:

All this comes to saying that the person of whom we say, 'He has pain' is, by the rules of the game, the person who cries, contorts his face, etc. The place of the pain—as we have said—may be in another person's body. If, in saying 'I', I point to my own body, I model the use of the word 'I' on that of the demonstrative 'This person' or 'He'. (*The Blue Book*, 68)

It seems that Wittgenstein is asking for the essential structure of the situation in which someone—myself or another person—is in pain. There are two different places where we might look for an answer. One is the connection between the physical damage and the sufferer's sensation and the other is the connection between his sensation and his response to it. The first connection is neurological,[37] while the second one is semantic. Wittgenstein's remark, that 'the place of the pain may be in another person's body', shows that his interest is in the semantic connection. That is why he says that 'the difference between the propositions "I have pain" and "He has pain" is not that of "L.W. has pain" and "Smith has pain". Rather it corresponds to the difference between moaning and saying that someone moans.'

We may well doubt, and in other contexts Wittgenstein himself often doubted, whether this kind of search for the essential structure of a situation is the best approach to a philosophical problem. But it seems certain that he adopted this approach to the question whether 'I' is a referential expression. The passage quoted above (*The Blue Book*, 68) continues with a very revealing analogy:

If, in saying 'I' I point to my own body, I model the use of the word 'I' on that of the demonstrative 'This person' or 'He'. (This way of making the two expressions similar is somewhat analogous to that which one sometimes adopts in mathematics, say in the proof that the sum of the three angles of a triangle is 180.)

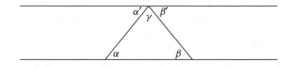

---

[37] It is discussed in detail in *Philosophical Remarks*, SS 57–66.

We say, $\alpha = \alpha'$ and $\beta = \beta'$ and $\gamma = \gamma$. The first two equalities are of an entirely different kind from the third. In 'I have pain', 'I' is not a demonstrative pronoun.

It is, of course, a personal pronoun, and what he is denying is that it has any referential force derived from the name of the person that it replaces. But his argument for this paradoxical denial is questionable. Why does he claim on p. 68 of *The Blue Book* that 'the mouth which says "I" or the hand that is raised to indicate that it is I who wish to speak or I who have toothache does not thereby point to anything'? Both these procedures present me to my audience as the target of my reference and, therefore as the target of their reference if they accept what I say and agree, 'Yes, you have toothache.' So why do these two procedures not amount to self-reference? This question elicits an unconvincing answer:

If in saying 'I' I point to my own body I model the use of the word 'I' on that of the demonstratives 'This person' or 'He'.  (*The Blue Book*, 68)

He calls this 'a way of *making* the two expressions similar' (my italicizing), and he uses the geometrical analogy sketched above to indicate that the similarity is superficial.

This argument depends on an implausible way of drawing the line between the essential and the accidental features of a situation in which someone says that he is in pain. First, it is not essential that he should be expressing rather than coolly reporting his pain. Second, and more important, even if the semantic connection between his words and his pain were necessarily expressive, there would be no reason to omit, as inessential, the connection between his pain and his body. So when Wittgenstein argues that the essential 'difference between "I have a pain" and "He has a pain" corresponds to the difference between moaning and saying that someone moans', he should have added that this difference is connected with another difference which has as good a claim to be essential: X's pain must be in X's body. It is irrelevant that we can imagine a world in which this was not necessarily so. It would be equally possible to imagine a world in which sufferers did not give vocal expression to their pains, but like beetles merely took silent action to avoid their causes.

It would even be possible to strengthen this objection to Wittgenstein's account of the essential difference between 'I have pain' and 'He has pain' by giving the screw another turn. We could say that the two features of the situation in which someone reports a pain are not only both essential but also directly connected with one another.

For it is because my pain is in my body that my body expresses it automatically without any need for any choice. But the point of this automatic link with expression would be lost if the pain itself were not connected, with equal necessity, with the damage done to my body.[38] It cannot, therefore, be right to treat the two features of the situation as two *independent* candidates for the title 'essential', nor can it be right to say that the basic difference between 'I have pain' and 'He has pain' corresponds to the difference between moaning and saying that someone is moaning; nor can it be right to say that 'If, in saying "I" I point to my own body, I model the use of the word "I" on that of the use of the demonstrative "This person" or "He", or to say that this is "a way of making two expressions similar.' Damn it all, it *is* me, by the usual criteria of personal identity.

If Wittgenstein's argument for the non-referentiality of 'I' is unsuccessful, is there anything else in his later work (post-1929) that would explain his paradoxical denial of its referentiality? Some commentators have suggested that it is a relic of the argument of the *Tractatus*. But that is very improbable. In his later work the question whether 'I' is a referential expression is a question about its use in daily life by embodied people, but in the *Tractatus*, the question was also, and often predominantly, a question about the nature of the residual ego within an embodied person. This made it as difficult to answer as it would be to run with an iron ball chained to one's ankle. So when Wittgenstein confined the question to the use of 'I' in daily life by embodied people, that, at least opened up the possibility of an agreed answer to it. But his own answer is too paradoxical for most commentators to accept.

[38] On this point, see Zettel, S, 540.

# Works of Wittgenstein Referred to in This Book

The number in the right hand column indicates the page on which the work is first mentioned.

TLP     *Tractatus Logico-Mathematicus*, tr. D. F. Pears and B. McGuin-     ix
        ness (Routledge, 1961)

Z       *Zettel*, ed. G. E. M. Anscombe and G. H. von Wright, tr.     39
        G. E. M. Anscombe (Blackwell, 1967)

# Index